D1758032

Purpose and Providence

2 8 MAY 2025

WITHDRAWN

York St John University

3 8025 00637409 7

1 2 JAN 1994

Purpose and Providence

Taking Soundings in Western Thought, Literature and Theology

Vernon White

YORK ST. JOHN
LIBRARY & INFORMATION
SERVICES

t&tclark

LONDON • NEW YORK • OXFORD • NEW DELHI • SYDNEY

T&T CLARK
Bloomsbury Publishing Plc
50 Bedford Square, London, WC1B 3DP, UK
1385 Broadway, New York, NY 10018, USA

BLOOMSBURY, T&T CLARK and the T&T Clark logo are
trademarks of Bloomsbury Publishing Plc

First published in Great Britain 2015
Paperback edition first published 2018

Copyright © Vernon White, 2015

Vernon White has asserted his right under the Copyright,
Designs and Patents Act, 1988, to be identified as Author of this work.

All rights reserved. No part of this publication may be reproduced or
transmitted in any form or by any means, electronic or mechanical,
including photocopying, recording, or any information storage or
retrieval system, without prior permission in writing from the publishers.

Bloomsbury Publishing Plc does not have any control over, or responsibility for,
any third-party websites referred to or in this book. All internet addresses
given in this book were correct at the time of going to press. The author and
publisher regret any inconvenience caused if addresses have changed or sites
have ceased to exist, but can accept no responsibility for any such changes.

A catalogue record for this book is available from the British Library.

Library of Congress Cataloging-in-Publication Data
White, Vernon, 1953-
Purpose and providence : taking soundings in western thought,
literature & theology / by Vernon White.
pages cm
Includes bibliographical references.
ISBN 978-0-567-66342-9 (hardback)
1. Providence and government of God–Christianity.
2. Meaning (Philosophy)–Religious aspects–Christianity. I. Title.
BT135.W43 2015
231'.5–dc23
2015017463

ISBN: HB: 978-0-567-66342-9
PB: 978-0-567-68250-5
ePDF: 978-0-567-66344-3
ePub: 978-0-567-66343-6

Typeset by Deanta Global Publishing Services, Chennai, India

To find out more about our authors and books visit
www.bloomsbury.com and sign up for our newsletters.

For my Godmother

Contents

Preface

I have been pondering purpose and providence for some time. Thirty years ago in the *The Fall of a Sparrow* I approached it chiefly through philosophical theology, focusing on the bare conceivability of a divine agent achieving particular purposes in the events of the world. Now I am revisiting some of these issues on a broader canvas.

As such there are obvious differences. I am more concerned here with whether and how we can actually identify divine purpose, as well as how we can conceive its possibility. This means engaging more with systematic theology, as well as re-imagining some previous philosophical approaches. I have also set the issues within a wider history of ideas, and explored them in engagement with literary works. In that sense this is more interdisciplinary offering.

There are also less easily defined differences. These have less to do with formal scope and method and more to do with overall texture, tone, priorities. Life experience, no doubt, accounts for this. Changing currents of thought also contribute. So too does the changing context of my working life over the years. All these have added to my appreciation of the issues at stake, and they all have their effect.

They have offered opportunity as well as inspiration. Sabbatical leave during my time at the Southern Theological Education and Training Scheme (STETS) helped kick-start this particular project. Latterly my role as Canon Theologian at Westminster Abbey, and the stimulus of the Theology department at King's College London, have provided further impetus. For these, and for the unfailing support and encouragement of my family, I am most grateful.

What has emerged? It is not a readily accessible and applicable public theology. Strictly speaking it is not public theology at all. It remains more speculative. But it is theology about issues which I still believe *matter* for both public and personal life. And that in the end is why I want to keep theology engaged with this area. A sense of purpose is critical to human being. So a theology of purpose must also, surely, deserve our attention.

Introduction: Something Lost and Found

I do not suppose I am unusual in being haunted by a sense of providence, even when it seems impossible to believe. I presume I am not alone because it inhabits so much of our shared Western sensibility, and beyond. It stalks our literature, our philosophy and our religion. It insinuates itself into the near-universal instinct for storytelling. Whenever we tell stories to make some sense of our life, or the life of the world, providence is almost always the ghost-writer. By providence I do not necessarily mean progress. Indeed I shall be making some sharp distinctions between providence and progress. But I do mean a sense that there is some purpose in the events of life, not just randomness. I also mean that we are not just creating this sense of purpose ourselves but finding it. Of course much of our purpose is self-created, but there is also the sense of a surplus of purpose beyond this. Something or Someone else is also making this story make sense, with us and for us. That is both the distinctive heart of the meaning of providence and its most problematic part. But it does not easily go away. Even when we think we have expelled it, relegated it the realms of superstition, fancy or false reasoning, it still finds a way of re-entering our world. That is why I talk of being haunted.

I am equally sure I am not alone in being haunted by a sense of its loss. This too has been a shared sensibility for many in Western culture, and beyond. We have lost a good deal of certainty about any objective purpose. We are not so sure as previous generations that events have meaning for us, certainly not divine meaning. This is usually (but not always) associated with loss of belief in God, certainly God as a personal agent. Such loss is part of the more general story told of the so-called disenchantment of the world. Often this is because of straightforward reductionism. With alternative explanations from the natural and social sciences, events no longer need divine will, purpose and causation to account for them. So explanations and interpretative frameworks for events are reduced to the 'purely' natural and human. These stories of the loss of meaning can be as seductive as stories of positive meaning. They seduce because they appeal to our pride: even if the loss is unwelcome, at least we have had the moral and intellectual courage to face up to it.

Yet these stories of disenchantment can themselves be as prone to the fancy and false reasoning they see in what they are rejecting. Stories about loss are often oversimplified to make them seem intelligible. In fact what seems like total loss may actually involve transference, displacement, transformation; what is lost may simply have precipitated new forms of itself. Hence the growing interest in some form of re-enchantment of the world, which now frequently appears across a range of literature. The early twentieth-century poet Rainer Rilke was a master of this re-enchantment. He presents images of transience and loss compellingly, but then recasts them in a different register: 'Why should decay be sadder than/ a fountain's return to its shimmering mirror?'.[1] Perhaps he is too optimistic – but he at least reminds us that loss may not be as total as it seems. Something different, even better, may be reformed out of it.

Another example of how disenchantment must not be oversimplified is well captured in Claire Tomalin's biography of the poet and novelist Thomas Hardy. It typifies in individual terms many of these features of secularization and disenchantment which are usually charted in wider social terms. She describes Hardy's experience like this:

> Losing faith in Christianity was like shedding a protective skin: intellectually necessary but also a melancholy process. … [He] arrived at his own conclusion with many fits starts and meanders, reluctant to let go of something that had absorbed so much of his imaginative life at the same time that he was eager to join the ranks of the enlightened. He felt the draining away of the old joyous certitudes as well as pride in the new clear thinking. This ambivalence made him into [someone] who in his later years still sometimes celebrated belief alongside disbelief. He could no longer believe, but he cherished the memory of belief.[2]

On the one hand this is a clear description of the process of losing faith and belief. There is an intellectual impetus to this, associated with new knowledge which appears to discredit religious belief, such as Darwinism. There is also

---

[1] Rainer Rilke, 'Transience', in Graham Good (trans.), *Rilke's Late Poetry* (Vancouver: Ronsdale Press, 2004), p. 124.
[2] Claire Tomalin, *Thomas Hardy: The Time-Torn Man* (London: Viking, 2006), p. 78.

a moral impetus, in the sense that we can take pride in having the courage to face reality without protective props. But on the other hand Tomalin is hinting that this is an oversimplification of the process. The trajectory is not straightforward. She is acknowledging at least a lingering wistfulness, and possibly a more radical ambivalence. She reminds us that later in life 'he still cherished the memory of belief', and even sometimes 'celebrated belief alongside disbelief'. So either the loss of faith is not total, or the new world view which replaces it not yet wholly convincing, or there are new forms of belief hinted, even in the absence of belief. Stories about the demise of providence all need to be examined in this light. They tend to oversimplification, and on closer scrutiny we may well find that providence can re-emerge from them, even if in different form.

My purpose in this essay is now to explore this dynamic. It is a review of the persistence of a sense of providence, especially in a robust theological form, in spite of its apparent loss. It also shows some re-imaginings of providence in the process.

A particular genre and scope

As such this will be, precisely and only, an essay with limited scope. So it is not a systematic survey of the doctrine of providence (nor of theological methodologies which might support it). It does not set out to review in detail all alternative models of God's relation to the world, or models of freewill and determinism. Nor does it attempt a close reading of any one theologian or religious philosopher (Spinoza, Hegel, Barth and others could all yield more than I take from them given closer reading). It is not even particularly concerned to expound or justify the content of providential purposes (e.g. by tackling Feuerbach's critique).[3] What *does* concern the essay is much more targeted. Rather than systematically reviewing either form or content, it is primarily concerned to display just the obstinate fact of this sense of universal and objective purpose; to demonstrate its character and conceivability largely

---

[3] Feuerbach's celebrated criticism was that the purpose of providence is always and necessarily self-serving. But this hardly needs any extensive response. Whatever its actual aberrations in practice in religion and theology, the alternative in principle is obvious: the goal of any divine providence worthy of the name is not to set conditions for human egoism, but for mutual love and justice.

through charting its resilience. To this end it tracks it in wider, literary experience, and especially in the tradition of non-reductionist Christian theology – and then also traces some more recent, re-imagined, shapes of it. It is, in other words, largely a (critical) mapping exercise, but with a very particular focus.

The structure

This will unfold in the following way. First, by some scene setting. The opening chapter offers some overall mapping from the history of Western thought to track where meaning and purpose generally has been found (and lost). It traces a path in which attitudes to time and history have changed, and shows how the *locus* of meaning has changed accordingly. It shows how teleology became rooted in historical process, first with God still conceived as the chief agent and goal, then with the autonomous human agent becoming more significant. In more recent trajectories of thought there has been less confidence in both the forward-moving narratives of history and the human self, and this too is noted. Nonetheless, meaning and purpose have persisted, and so their sources and 'drivers' have to be uncovered more carefully. In this context I take note especially of a recent philosophical survey of the history of providence, *Providence Lost* by Genevieve Lloyd.[4] This is an elegant account of human interaction with ideas of both impersonal necessity and divine purpose. The loss regretted here is not so much the loss of our sense of engagement with the will of a personal God, but the loss of a more Stoic and Spinozan recognition of necessity. Lloyd hopes that at least something of this Spinozan sense of a necessary external ordering of events can be recovered, even without a theistic or other transcendent metaphysical basis. Meaning, she thinks, can at least persist there.

Alongside this I also refer to Charles Taylor's monumental and multi-layered analysis in *A Secular Age*.[5] Taylor's discussion of providence has a broader field of reference. He does not have the same targeted focus on issues of freedom and necessity. He sets the issue of providence in a wider frame:

---

[4] Genevieve Lloyd, *Providence Lost* (Cambridge, MA: Harvard University Press, 2008).
[5] Charles Taylor, *A Secular Age* (Cambridge, MA: Harvard University Press, 2007).

in particular, our changing conceptions of transcendence, human fulfilment and moral motivation. It is this wider canvas which then helps him chart the processes of secularization not just as the subtraction of certain beliefs, but their transmutation. Within the process of disenchantment Taylor identifies a number of 'cross pressures' which resist the confinement of a purely immanent frame of reference in life and hint at transcendent realities, perhaps even transcendent agency. This leads to a more general exploration of what he calls the 'obstinate presence' of meaning and mattering. The intrinsic authority of narrative helps display this. Even more telling are the imperatives of value and moral motivation. These can move even the atheist or agnostic to metaphysical wonder and a sense of objective purpose which is hard to contain in the immanent frame. I find this expressed especially well in a short, sharp, suggestive essay by Simon Critchley.[6]

The next chapter moves on from intellectual history to take soundings in a different way. It charts similar stories of loss and transformation in literary accounts. This changes the focus from shifting belief to shifting experience. But they are interrelated and this will become apparent. The two main literary sources I consider are chosen as exemplars of honesty, especially about the sense of loss and absence. They are writers who describe unflinchingly the texture of experience without belief in God or divine purpose. One describes the experience from within the process of losing faith, the other from the context of never having had a faith to lose. Both, however, also show the signs of 'presence' as well as absence. In different ways they both reinforce the persistence of a displaced sense of transcendent purpose, even from within a fundamentally faithless world view. So in that sense they provide a telling test: they display a persistence of purpose right at the heart of a story about its absence.

I have already trailed the first – Thomas Hardy, a voice from the late 19th and early twentieth century. His writing offers a fertile field to explore both the loss of a sense of providence, but also the impossibility of absolutizing that loss. So on the one hand we find him profoundly influenced by many of the apparently secularizing influences of his time, notably the theory of evolution. On the other hand, Hardy's godless and evolutionary world still displays

---

[6] Simon Critchley, *Infinitely Demanding: Ethics of Commitment, Politics of Resistance* (London: Verso, 2007).

internal contradictions, signs of some kind of transcendent meaning. Even in the absence of God, the world which he saw revealed at least some presence of unaccountable value, agency and purpose. This obstinate presence even in absence (of both God and providence) trails more than a trace of late-modern irony, I will suggest.

The other writer is Julian Barnes from the twenty-first century, who explores this absence even more radically: that is, not as one who has lost a presence but one who never knew it in the first place. He writes from a place of more radical uncertainty about *all* knowledge, moral and scientific as well as religious. All knowing and being is slippery, there is nothing but 'great unrest'.[7] He shows us the texture of experience in a world in which it is not just difficult to grasp truth, meaning and purpose, but virtually impossible. Yet this isn't necessarily a retreat to wholesale constructivism and anti-realism as if there really are no (moral) truths of history and personal life to be found at all. For although he shows history deconstructed, randomised and fruitless, he also finds it displaying strange and significant resonances and repeated themes, as if it can tell us something after all. Likewise, although he displays personal identity as fractured, he still represents love as something profound and 'objectively' purposive. Here too, like Hardy, we find at least the shadows of a transcendent meaning and purpose.

The next section turns to theology. Here the main drivers of purpose which were identified in intellectual history (i.e. the senses of necessity, narrative, moral determination, transcendence) are tracked in theological doctrines of divine will and sovereignty, embodied in 'classical' doctrines of providence. This entails a brief theological history of some well-trodden paths: that is, tracing notions of providence from biblical origins through Augustine, Medieval and Reformation exponents (especially Aquinas and Calvin), through to the twentieth century and beyond (especially Barth, Frei and, more briefly, liberal and postmodern contributors). One simple conclusion of telling the theological story in this way is that it demonstrates the sheer persistence of a doctrine of objective (divine) purpose in the events of this world. In that sense it mirrors the more general sense of purpose tracked in intellectual history and literary experience. In particular, it shows this persistence specifically in the robust form of the doctrine. That is, it demonstrates a continuing thread of belief

---

[7] A phrase from his novel *The Sense of an Ending* (London: Jonathan Cape, 2011).

that God is *universally* and *effectively* active in providence, creating meaning in particular events as well as in overall outcomes. This has endured in spite of the countervailing claims of human autonomy, secularism or disenchantment. This persistence does not mean all issues have been resolved. Far from it – any theology of providence predicated on a radically sovereign and good God acting as a personal agent will struggle with recurring issues of how to conceive divine causality, and how to maintain a credible narrative of purpose in the face of the actual empirical realities which unfold – especially the reality of evil. So these issues too are noted throughout, and marked out for further treatment.

The shape of the next chapter then follows. It is a critical review of recent trajectories within theology where providence is specifically re-imagined to address these issues. So here I note first how conceptual issues about causality are currently being dealt with in philosophical theology and scientific theology, and outline some new models being proposed. Then, because of our incredulity towards metanarrative, I note how contemporary theologians can offer a more open-textured account of divine action and purpose: a providence of many possible histories and 'shapes of freedom', rather than one overall narrative.[8] I refer especially to the notion of figural relationships between events, building on Barth and Frei: that is, the possibilities of seeing a patterned family resemblance between events, even though there is little or no visible causal relationship between them. This provides a framework for conceiving God's action in the many histories favoured by late modernity, yet retaining a real and ultimate connectedness. It shows how these histories can be purposively connected without imposing any artificial meaning or easily identifiable *telos*, and without needing to find any single causal chain to link them. It offers a picture of providence which offers a sense of redemptive purpose in all things, but without requiring an unrealistic doctrine of visible progress. It affirms divine redemptive purpose in both particulars and overall outcomes, but without needing to defend dubious claims to interpret it confidently. The pivot and pattern of all this is the Christ event of cross and resurrection – itself a narrative of presence and purpose in everything, yet one in which moments of absence and bewilderment are also fully acknowledged. Because none of this

[8] 'Shapes of freedom' is a phrase from Peter C. Hodgson, *God in History: Shapes of Freedom* (Minneapolis: Fortress Press, 1989).

will work without a notion of radical transcendence to undergird it, this too is emphasized and explored – I present it as a necessary basis of both divine causality and divine redemption.

In both these chapters, the overall theology which emerges is displayed as much as argued – there is no claim to have decisively dismissed other options. So, for example, the option of reconceiving God without such radical transcendence, sovereignty, omniscience and far-reaching action, is well noted but not fully pursued and refuted. This is simply because my major concern is to see whether a re-imagined but radical and robust providence *can* still be displayed. If this is possible, then there is simply no need for theology to compromise so much in other areas.

Nonetheless the credibility of this picture will always need further testing. So that leads to the final chapter where I refer back to scripture and experience to test further the credibility of what has been displayed. Here the pattern of providence proposed is strained back through the sieve of scripture and experience. In particular I ask how credible it is in the face of extreme experiences of evil, where a sense of purpose is not just absent but morally impossible to conceive. I claim no new answers here. I offer no theodicy because I suspect none is possible. I simply try to clarify, as far as possible, what this picture of providence actually entails for God's relation to evil, and compare it with what alternative accounts entail. I also test its credibility in praxis. I ask what sort of praxis displays this sort of belief. What I suggest is that it cannot be authentically displayed in action predicated on linear progress – but it can be displayed in prayer and all other political, ecclesial, personal action which presuppose an ultimate purpose without this sort of progress.

A definite proposal

What this offers overall by no means claims to be a definitive picture. It is more a collage of possibilities by which providence is sustained. It is a texture of thought and experience about providence, rather than a tightly defined system of belief; an inevitable consequence of acknowledging the sense of loss as well as its persistence. But precisely as such I believe this makes it more credible, not less. Providence without any intervening modes of loss has been too thin, too easily assimilated to facile views of progress and so too easily discredited. Whereas providence which embraces different shapes and allows for a good deal of apophaticism is thicker. It offers a richer vein of theology, and so will be more convincing.

In the end, then, the tenor of this essay is still fundamentally positive. For all that its proposals emerge from persuasive stories of loss, they are not overwhelmed by them. They look for, and affirm, an enduring presence in the absence. Belief in providence has been described as both necessary and impossible and in this essay I fully acknowledge both.[9] But it is the necessity, finally, which drives me more than the impossibility. It is, still, the haunting presence which persuades me most, not the absence. It is the surplus of meaning and purpose we encounter which grips my imagination, as much as the meaning we create for ourselves.

---

[9] Tim Gorringe, *God's Theatre: A Theology of Providence* (London: SCM Press, 1991).

1

Mapping Meaning and Purpose: A Brief History of Ideas

Where can meaning and purpose be found? Meaning and purpose are correlative terms. They belong together, at least in the sense that I shall usually refer to them. That is to say, the sort of meaning I mean is what we experience when we find both pattern and purpose, especially in relation to a wider world. Put another way, when a relation to a wider pattern is fulfilled purposively, whether in moral, aesthetic or utilitarian modes, that is how we find meaning.

But where is this specifically purposive meaning most persuasive? Where does it become most apparent? How can it be mapped?

There are many ways to track this, and ultimately it is the theological way which most interests me. But I will not begin there in any detail. I want first to offer a brief account of it from the background of a more general (Western) history of ideas. I will draw on the commentary of social philosophers to explore the question within a complex weave of other issues. There we find that the location and relocation of meaning and purpose mutates, diachronically and synchronically, depending on wider changing perceptions of freedom and necessity, time and history, and the self, as well as on theological views about God. We see there how purpose has had to navigate increasing secularism, pluralism and scepticism about the possibilities of any sort of belief in objective meanings. Equally what this background mapping shows, I believe, is its persistence, in spite of its mutations and displacements. It shows its underlying drivers. And so, because theology speaks out of this more general background, as well as to it, it is important to review it. It maps the context in which theology operates.

The turn to history

One useful guide to this shifting location of meaning has been provided by Michael Gillespie.[1] He charts one major reorientation in particular. It came, unsurprisingly, with the onset of modernity. It is the turn to history. Pre-modern humanity, says Gillespie, did not find meaning by looking backwards or forwards (i.e. to the past or future) but upwards and downwards (i.e. to eternity and our current relation to it). We defined ourselves then by our location in land, race and eternity, but not so much by our place in time and history. Only more recently, in modernity, have we come to conceive ourselves more readily in an historical narrative. In this new orientation we look for meaning in the process of moving forward in time. We are also more inclined to see ourselves as an essential part of the process: we help *make* the narrative and move it forward. As such we assume human autonomy within this process, and so meaning has come to depend critically on our freedom to act within history.

Naturally this generalizes. There are counter examples to these overall characterizations of both pre-modernity and modernity.[2] Nonetheless, allowing for a broad brush, the overall picture can still be painted. Thus to fill it out further, we can characterize the pre-modern era as a time when forward-moving narrative was less significant because cycles of time were marked more by seasons and festivals. This tends to show that meaning was being found more a historically in underlying 'eternal' spiritual realities, with purpose generated less through the linear movement of time and more through recurring cycles of events which mediated truths and realities beyond time to which we might aspire. In popular culture this associated with pagan ritual, rooted in the experience of natural cycles of birth and death, and in the Western philosophical tradition it connected readily with Platonic thought. By contrast, in the modern era, when meaning and purpose was largely transferred to the narrative of development within time, routines and cycles

---

[1] Michael Allen Gillespie, *The Theological Origins of Modernity* (London: University of Chicago Press, 2008).

[2] For example, alongside pre-modernity's general tendency to the 'vertical' there were also medieval millennial groups looking forward to specifically historical fulfilments of their hopes. Conversely, modernity's overall inclination to historical process (and progress) has to reckon with the more 'vertical' transcendent instincts of, for example, romanticism, and the more pessimistic narratives of some Pietism.

have become less marked. Where they persisted they have tended only to serve that overall process of development. The real substance of meaning has now been relocated within the forward temporal movement itself, and purpose is found as we contribute actively to that development.

This is why modernity – though not late modernity – has tended to see the purpose of 'progress' as the more natural goal, a movement towards a better state or fulfilling endpoint. Particular moments within such stories can still have special meaning, but that derives precisely from their role in moving the story forward to this end in particularly significant ways. This historicized view of meaning received some of its greatest impetus in nineteenth-century philosophical and theological traditions, especially Hegel and Marx.

History, purpose and God

There is evidence of this turn to history in the way it correlated with changing conceptions of God (even though it did not in itself always depend on God). Thus in the pre-modern sensibility a broadly Platonic conception of God naturally flourished: that is, a God conceived as a non-temporal a historical source of ultimate meaning. In the reflective theology of Western Christianity this found systematic expression in classical theism, emphasizing divine eternity and changelessness. It was a natural fit with a sensibility orientated towards cyclical and eternal realities. But with the shift to history in modernity a more dynamic and narrative conception of God tended to emerge. This too has been a natural fit. Where historical narrative is the main site of meaning, God is more readily conceived as an engaged, responsive, agent within the historical process. This God also sits more comfortably with the personalistic and narrative basis of biblical theology, rather than with the tenets of classical theism.

Personalistic theism of this kind also helped give some substantive content to the teleology of history. It meant that the goal could easily be defined specifically as the 'kingdom' or 'personal rule' of this God. It has been variously conceived. It could stand both within history and at the end of it; its fulfilment could be conceived either at various moments within the temporal sequence, or at the end of it, or both. Either way, history could remain the important site of meaning. It was the natural environment in which God's personal rule could be worked out towards that kingdom – whether through proximate or final ends. The influence of Neoplatonism was not entirely expunged in this changing theological view of history; some notion of a transcendent and eternal City of God remained – not least through Augustine's abiding influence. But even that appeal to transcendence has often functioned to safeguard history as God's theatre of concern, not to diminish it – for it helped guard against the sort of apocalypticism that foreshortens historical reality altogether.[3]

History, purpose, the absence of God – and the turn to self

Of course, this correlation between God and purposive history broke down altogether in later modernity. That is the familiar story of secularization and disenchantment, where God is simply removed as a significant agent or explanation. For some, notably John Milbank (as well as Gillespie), the seeds of this were sown a long way back. The culprit was the medieval shift from scholastic realism to nominalism. This entailed a move away from notions of a hierarchy of being and the philosophy of analogy by which God and the rest of reality could be related. This in turn eroded the overall significance of God in relation to this world. For where God can no longer be conceived as the highest form of being, connected analogously to other forms of lesser being, the scene is set for removing God altogether from the world. This severing was reinforced by voluntarist views of God which detached God from the grasp of the ordinary reason and known being. So when reason then advanced in the 17th and 18th centuries it had the space to deal with the created world order in its own terms, unfettered by God.

---

[3] Cf. Peter Hodgson's estimation: on the one hand the two Cities are distinct, the one 'living like an alien' in the other, without any real historical change in the relationship envisaged; but on the other hand God is still 'guiding the heavenly city to its consummation': Hodgson, *God in History*, pp. 17, 18. Cf. also R. Bittner, 'Augustine's Philosophy of History', in G. Matthews (ed.), *The Augustinian Tradition* (Berkeley: University of California Press, 1999), pp. 345–60. Referring to *De Vera Religione* (7.13) he points out that Augustine clearly saw history, as distinct from philosophy, as the sphere of God's providential activity, and the source of our knowledge of it.

There are other more nuanced ways of telling this story. In Charles Taylor's hands the new 'social imaginary' of secularism is ascribed to a more complex interweaving of many multifarious elements, such as religious wars, Black Death, ecclesiastical corruption, not just the nominalist shift and subsequent rise of scientific method;[4] Taylor also draws more attention to the ambiguities of the secularization itself. Yet the consequence is much the same: God is still largely cleared from the field of history.

However, it is notable that history itself remained significant. It did not cease to be a site of meaning and purpose just because God was removed as its main driver. In fact, if anything, the release of history from the eschatological constraints of Christian theology has actually deepened the development of its own immanent meanings and narrative purpose. For, as Taylor puts it, the 'story' of history which is no longer the story of the kingdom of God can now be the purpose of 'Progress', 'Reason and Freedom', 'Civilization', 'Decency' or 'Human Rights'.[5] Of these progress in particular has dominated, easily reoccupying in secular form the old theological view of divine purpose in events.[6]

What made this possible? One cause, of course, was the increasing turn to the autonomous agent and the self to replace God as the main generator of this purpose. History may no longer have God driving it (nor any other metaphysical basis), but it still has us – so we take centre stage to help further that progress. Human autonomy, and ultimately the human self, now create purpose in history and move it forward, even if that is only an immanent purpose. Thus Gillespie again:

> With the development of a new notion of human will and freedom … the time in which humans lived, that is history, appeared in a new light. The relevant story of humanity from this perspective was not the cyclical pattern the ancients imagined, nor the biblical story of a past fall and future (divine) redemption in God's new kingdom, nor even the humanistic account of man's Sisyphean efforts to master *fortuna*, but the story of humanity's ever increasing conquest and transformation of the natural world. History in this way came to be seen as the story of human progress. …[7]

---

4   Taylor, *A Secular Age.*
5   Ibid., p. 716.
6   Gillespie, *Theological Origins of Modernity*, p. 12.
7   Ibid., p. 281.

In short, when meaning and purpose was no longer found in symbolic relationships rooted in the being or action of God, it simply transferred to the human creation of meaning through our own finite being or action.

To be sure, this is not necessarily sustainable. As more weight is put on the role of human autonomy and subjectivity, in all areas of life and knowledge, its own limits become exposed. And I shall return to that. But for the moment we just need to register this basic trajectory. With and without God, historical process became and remained a main site for meaning, and one of its main drivers appears to be the human self. So this is certainly part of the weave we now inherit in later modernity – along with echoes of those earlier more cyclical sources of meaning.

Current trajectories: Problematics of progress and the travails of *telos*

The next question, however, now follows – is this still the case? Do we still have this confidence in history and its forward-moving trajectory as our main site of meaning? Are we still wedded to this sort of progress? Are we still confident in ourselves as prime movers? Or have we already now moved into yet another era, with different perspectives?

Identifying the trends of any era is never easy. No era stands alone with a self-sufficient sensibility. 'Pre-modernity' and 'modernity' have both proved notoriously porous notions, even considered in retrospect. So it will be even more difficult to assess the sensibility in which we still currently stand. Nonetheless, some commentators are willing to try. And some at least are clear: while accepting that historical progress has, as a matter of fact, become dominant, they nonetheless think it has now become discredited and questionable; they claim our quest for meaning there has now stalled.

Polemicist John Gray, for example, tells the story like this.[8] He first echoes some of Gillespie's analysis. History did indeed become a source for meaning especially because Christianity introduced teleology into history, propagating

---

[8] John Gray, *Black Mass: Apocalyptic Religion and the Death of Utopia* (London: Penguin, 2007). This radical questioning of progress is not universal, however: it still has champions. See, for example, Steven Pinker, *The Better Angels of our Nature* (London: Allen Lane, 2011). On progress, see further below, Chapter 5, pp. 156–8.

the belief that the purposes of 'salvation' are to be found within it. Under the influence of Augustine's Platonism this was not a facile doctrine of progress; however, it did help set the scene for it. For what Gray also emphasizes is the way processes of secularization then appropriated this teleological foundation. When secular political ideologies, parasitic on Christianity's sense of overall teleology, replaced the Christian metanarrative and metaphysics these not only reinforced teleology in general but also turned it into naked doctrines of progress.

For Gray this is what has also discredited them. It is precisely when such secular ideologies – Marxism, scientism, liberalism – defined their teleology too crudely in terms of a progress that they have been falsified. None has proved that it can resolve our conflicts, and none has delivered the utopia it promises.[9] Worse, many try to impose it violently. In other words, 'progress' simply has not materialized – not in any terms that we might normally use for it. Instead, the drive to progress has just highlighted the hidden cost and tyranny of teleology itself – leaving Gray sceptical about all historical process as a reliable source of meaning. Indeed, he wants 'freedom from *all* narrative' – at least when it is used as a tool of progressive teleology (and if religion is to be credible it must acknowledge this, re-presenting itself more as a way of mystery rather than implicating itself again in historical teleology).

Other commentators share some of this analysis but also dig deeper.[10] Thus, for Charles Taylor, the root of our current quest for meaning is not just empirical disenchantment with progress. It is a deeper disenchantment with all 'explanation', especially overall explanation. Lyotard's seminal essay *The Postmodern Condition* pinpointed the heart of this now familiar thesis. Late modernity is a world-weary condition in which all big stories fail to convince because they fail to have adequate explanatory power. The stories of science, religion and political ideology have not succeeded because none has managed to legitimate our knowledge in a decisive way. This leads to various epicycles of displaced meaning. It has shifted meaning and purpose into other areas i.e. the turn to the self – but still without any underlying story to support them.

---

[9]   The only ideology not so discredited, for Gray, is Spinoza's 'de-politicized' view of salvation, but this was in any case an acceptance of the necessity of things, rather than a narrative of redemption.

[10]   Cf. especially Charles Taylor, *Sources of the Self* (Cambridge: Cambridge University Press, 1989) and *A Secular Age*; cf. also Alasdair MacIntyre, *After Virtue* (London: Duckworth, 1981) and *Whose Justice? Which Rationality?* (London: Duckworth, 1988).

This in turn has led to consequences in our general quest for meaning which go beyond the demise of progress alone. If all overall explanations, whether metaphysical or narrative, are suspect, then there is no obvious structure to support deep meaning of any kind. To have no goals or *telos* set by overarching or transcendent realities, whether these are purposive historicism or Platonic ideals of eternity, drains all motivation and meaning.

The alternative is this turn to the human self, in order to create goals for ourselves. But is this trajectory in fact any more secure? It is unlikely. As Taylor points out, commitment, meaning and purpose can become even harder to sustain when goals are only self-created, self-referential and therefore limited. This is because the self is itself less secure. It is no longer so clearly defined; self and the rest of reality interpenetrate. So this fluidity of the self and its boundaries adds immeasurably to our overall perplexity about where we can find meaning and purpose.[11] The spectre of total meaninglessness may then begin to haunt.

This analysis of Taylor's goes beyond political and social questions to the very meaning of meaning itself, so it is a more multilayered account than Gray's. Nonetheless, the same core issues are still identified. Both Gray and Taylor are describing a current context in which linear, forward-moving historicism no longer easily convinces. So in these terms at least, we are certainly being told that we have moved into a different mind-set. We inhabit a world in which any purpose mediated through metaphysics, progressive public history or even the self's own endeavours, is open to question. Confidence in all meanings and purposes found in pre-modernity and modernity has eroded – and there seems little reliable to replace them.

Such an analysis can be supported by data from a wide range of sources. Within 'high' culture of art and literature there is the phenomenon of endless unanswered questions and unresolved deconstruction. There is the pervasive art of constant deferral of any form of closure, resolution, final explanation (one example of this in the writing of Julian Barnes will be explored in more detail later). Within popular consumer culture there is the corresponding phenomenon of self-defeating, self-referential, laws of diminishing returns; a feverish but directionless activity where meaning is sought in consumer

---

[11] In Weber's terms, a purely self-referential world view may easily become a prison: but we could just as easily say it is a prison without walls. Either way, it is not a secure basis for meaning.

pleasures without any realistic end in view. Either way these are symptoms of this new culture: that is, one in which the currency of *telos* has been devalued, historicism is suspect and meaning itself is called into question.

Further trajectories: The paradoxical persistence of purpose

So there has indeed been loss here, of a kind. Yet, as I have intimated, that is by no means the whole picture. For Taylor has also pointed out that notions of development and purpose, even if they shift and change, still retain extraordinary residual power. The instinct for historical development and teleology persists, even when its metaphysical or empirical props seem to have been removed or compromised. These are what Taylor calls 'cross pressures'. And these too still form part of the current mind-set.

This staying power of objective purpose had already been demonstrated in the past. The Black Death, the 100 Years War, medieval corruption and the philosophical shift to nominalism, might easily have robbed history of any credible sense of order meaning. They did not. Liberal progressive historicism still developed. As already noted, the demise of God and secularization did not remove it either. Teleology was simply displaced onto other ideologies.

A similar resilience has been demonstrated more recently. True, it has been severely tested again in these deconstructions of late modernity; there has been the powerful cumulative effect of two world wars, the Holocaust, 9/11, post-modern criticism of corrupt power and reason. All these certainly challenged facile readings of a linear progressive history and corroded faith in easy big stories of progress (whether religious or secularized). But again, they still have not stripped history of all teleology. The evidence lies, for example, in the pragmatics of political culture, the rhetoric of political discourse in which the rationale for political activity almost always includes appeal to some better future state, rather than steady state. This persists even when normal indicators of growth in the economy or social capital appear to suggest they are unsustainable. The continued pursuit of education, of welfare, of personal fulfilment, is all predicated on some sense that a goal lies 'ahead'. In other words, further chapters are always still being envisaged.

This persistence is a feature of theory, not just practice: the very critique of progress that postmodernity offers actually reinforces, paradoxically, a kind of narrative structure of development because it implies it has moved to a 'better' perspective. In its claim that we have now moved on beyond religious and secular metanarratives into a post-narrative phase, that sense of a 'next stage' is in fact restating a quasi-teleological narrative. So while it is easy, with Gray and others, to deplore and discredit all particular specific narratives of progress, it is much harder to deny that some general sense of meaning through movement and development still persists. Narratives with a goal still have power to convey meaning even when the substantive meaning they purport to convey may easily be debunked in particular circumstances. Their underlying structure of teleological meaning remains resilient, even when their actual outcome appears to deny it.

This raises a key question. If some sense of teleology persists, outlasting the support both of religion and secular stories, what is its origin? Is it just human autonomy that accounts for it? Are purely self-referential goals adequate to motivate and sustain deep meaning after all? Or is there some other power of fate, necessity or destiny, which creates these goals? This is not just a question of human psychology, but of metaphysics and ontology. We need to ask not just where this human sense of purpose persists in the mind, but whether this sense has any ground in the structure of reality outside our minds. What are the ultimate grounds of our persistent sense of meaning and objective purpose? What is driving the self to posit such meaning and purpose?

Meaning in necessity as well as freedom: *Providence Lost* and the story of gods and philosophers

One such driver of objective meaning and purpose is necessity. *Prima facie* this might seem odd. What is imposed on us, either by the gods, God, or by the impersonal structures of reality, might seem to close down meaning. But in fact it can function in the opposite way. The pressure of necessity can be felt not just as an arbitrary constraint but as a stimulus to provoke response. As the frame of a picture focuses more clearly what lies within it, a measure of necessity can generate meaning by providing parameters to sharpen meaning;

these parameters provide a frame to help interpret what is there, why it is there, and to channel our energies more effectively within them.

This sort of significance in necessity has been well recognized by Genevieve Lloyd in *Providence Lost*.[12] The book overall is a genealogy of the notion of providence, charting various different origins and meanings of beliefs and dispositions which have sheltered under the name. But its focus might just as easily be described as the genealogy of its closely related notions of freedom and necessity. These are the key players for Lloyd, jostling throughout history in uneasy tension, a framework to help interpret the shifting meanings of providence, to help locate meaning and account for its persistence. And as we shall see, for Lloyd it is necessity which proves just as important as freedom.

Lloyd begins her review with Euripides and the Stoics, their positive sense of a necessity imposed by the gods and by notions of a higher order of justice and cosmic necessity. It was a pervasive and influential world view. It was widely believed that purpose was consistently and inexorably being worked out through the operation of 'fate', a cosmic purpose operating through natural laws to some moral end.[13]

To be sure, it was also challenged. The Epicureans rejected any sense of cosmic design in favour of a more invigorating sense of personal responsibility. So Lloyd spends some time in these debates of the ancient world, before her main discussion of the later and similar debate between Spinoza and Descartes at the cusp of modernity. In both cases there was confrontation between a world view of overall necessity (where freedom is conceived as a willing convergence with necessity) and a free human will.

This story is complex and the balance of forces constantly shifts. But it is always the presence of some element of necessity which helps shape meaning and purpose. This isn't immediately apparent. The autonomous will and its freedom appears to become most significant as modernity dawns – especially with Descartes[14] – so freedom has tended to be presented as the primary

---

[12] See above p. 4. Lloyd's book is a lucid essay, deserving wide recognition.

[13] Cf. Seneca's expression of this view in *De Providentia*.

[14] Lloyd's account of Descartes draws on J. Cottingham, R. Stoothoff and D. Murdoch (trans.), *The Philosophical Writings of Descartes* (Cambridge: Cambridge University Press, 1985) and L. M. Baker (ed.), *The Letters of Elizabeth of Bohemia* (London: The Bodley Head, 1953); also Carola Oman, *Elizabeth of Bohemia* (London: Hodder & Stoughton, 1938).

sphere where meaning and purpose are most obviously located. Yet as Lloyd notes, the greater the weight placed on this sphere, the greater too was the human predicament of anxiety and vulnerability within it as the human subject struggles to establish its scope (and often deluded itself in the process). This leads the human self either to act hubristically or to be crushed with an over-developed sense of responsibility. Inevitably, the self's own boundaries then change, adding to its sense of insecurity. As such we have only limited resources to interpret the misfortunes which necessity, the uncontrollable element of life, hurls at us. If, like Descartes, we believe the uncontrollable is the providence of a benevolent God then these misfortunes may still have some meaning, however opaque – and however challenging that is for theodicy. If we do not interpret this with God we are left more vulnerable, with a large domain of meaninglessness. But either way we still have the anxiety of contingency: does this misfortune mean we have not exercised our own freedom enough? Could we have done more? *And so in the end we return to some frame of necessity to provide meaning.* For at least this will help set the terms to deal with the destabilizing contingency and freedom that we seek.

Lloyd appeals especially to Spinoza to substantiate this. For although Spinoza grants some sense of freedom, it is not presented as a sphere beyond the necessary and uncontrollable. Rather, for Spinoza, it lies largely within the mind's willing embrace of the necessary.[15] This makes meaning for the self much less precarious, and purpose more steadfast. It also makes the divine will more comprehensible, because the mind's willing embrace of necessity is pre-eminently the case for God's own being. That follows from conceiving God's will to be inseparable from God's intellect: that is, God's grasp of what is necessarily the case.

In fact the underlying theology here is problematic. It means, amongst other things, that God would not be conceived as 'doing' particular things as an exercise of God's free will: God simply wills universally what is a necessity. As such God would apparently have no concern for particular ends within the whole, for what God 'does' (i.e. wills) is the whole, not any 'part'. Yet the main point can stand without these particular theological implications. A more

---

[15] Lloyd's account of Spinoza draws on E. M. Curley (ed.), *The Collected Works of Spinoza* (Princeton: Princeton University Press, 1985), and A. Wolf (ed.), *The Correspondence of Spinoza* (London: Frank Cass, 1966).

stable sense of meaning and purpose can be found if we are prepared to accept the necessities of the whole (whether or not we leave God and ourselves some freedom to arrange its parts).

To be sure, in terms of the usual story line, Spinoza's embrace of necessity did not win the day. He did not become the dominant influence for modernity. Instead the course of modernity was more significantly shaped by Descartes, with a belief in the autonomous human will as the most determinative source of meaning. This is not surprising. The intrinsic limits of individual autonomy (imposed by survival, chance, illness, mortality) become masked in modernity by the greater collective possibilities of technology. That is why the supposed capacity of the autonomous will to control and generate meaning largely triumphed.[16]

However, Lloyd herself is not persuaded by this apparently triumphant trajectory. So she reminds us again how the autonomous will is precarious and limited, and emphasizes how this was even true for Descartes. Even he never actually had an absolute doctrine of human autonomy, in spite of his preoccupation with it. Instead, following Augustine, he always had to conceive the human will in relation to the constraints of divine will and purposes, as well as the world's own necessities. Descartes also had to accept the will's limitations in the face of the passions (nicely exposed in his personal correspondence with the Princess Elisabeth of Bohemia – recounted in one of Lloyd's most illuminating detours).

Lloyd also develops the point more generally, stressing the intrinsic limits of any human autonomy in any context where it is absolutized. She points out that whenever meaning is sought primarily in what is humanly controllable, meaning itself has become disorientated by the void in which it operates. This is one of the consequences of losing belief in providence in a Cartesian world which prizes freedom. Because of the intrinsic instability of the human self it leaves us with no secure source of meaning at all and we are left in an even greater void. Thus 'the fate of the Cartesian will has been to outlive the model of providence that once made it emotionally viable'.[17] Lloyd here is effectively echoing the analysis of much so-called postmodernity already noted: that

---

[16] Lloyd, *Providence Lost*, p. 307.
[17] Ibid., p. 308.

is, the collapse of supporting metanarrative makes all meaning problematic particularly when it places too much strain on the self.

The implications of this for Lloyd are not a return to the necessities of objective divine purpose represented by theism and divine providence. For her there is no credible return to religious belief. But she is suggesting we recover more sympathy for the largely rejected position of Spinoza and the Stoics before him (Leibniz and Kant likewise are enlisted in support). Here, she believes, we can regain a sense of meaning in the uncontrollable, the necessities which govern life (especially the whole of life, not just the part we think we are playing).[18] Meaning will arise precisely in identifying these necessities, in freely accepting them, then participating responsibly within them. In this way freedom will converge with necessity rather than fighting vainly against it. And it is this which will provide a more secure and tenacious source of (ethical) meaning – more convincing than either exalting the autonomous will or engaging the will with an outmoded belief in divine providence.

This is not a route I can follow wholesale. The inconsistency lies in refusing any religious or metaphysical basis for this necessity. Lloyd appeals to Spinoza but does not seem to realize that he cannot easily be secularized in the way she would like. As she herself explains it, Spinoza's own conjunction of freedom and necessity, and the meaning this generates, depended on their unique unity in God – but this is at odds with the sort of overall secularization she has adopted. Nor can she easily appeal to an entirely secularized Stoic sense of necessity without similar inconsistency. That too normally rests on some sort of metaphysical faith: that is, the impersonal notion of 'cosmic' justice.[19] So there is something of an internal contradiction here when she appeals to necessity. It requires a religious or metaphysical basis, but she is reluctant to offer it.

This contradiction is demonstrated in Lloyd's own illustration of necessity from Euripides' final play *Iphigenia at Aulis*. Iphigenia finds meaning in freely accepting the necessity of her death, in order to free the becalmed Greek

---

[18] Cf. Lloyd's use of Kant: 'Individual men and even entire nations little imagine that, while they are pursuing their own ends, each in his own way, and often in opposition to others, they are unwittingly guided in their advance along a course intended by nature' (Kant's *Political Writings*, p. 41). Cited in Lloyd, *Providence Lost*, p. 289.

[19] Cf. Stephen Mulhall, 'To bear necessity' (*Times Literary Supplement* review, January 2010).

fleet. By welcoming this, her dying 'enacts the appropriation of necessity – the transformation of fate into freedom'.[20] But how far is this sense of satisfied meaning due simply to the 'free' acceptance of necessity per se, and how much is due to the belief that it is death in a good cause, a greater good? If the latter then there is no intrinsic delight or meaning in accepting necessity as such, only certain kinds of necessity which belong to a wider metaphysical and moral scheme. Yet for Lloyd there is no way back to the specific metaphysics and religious beliefs of Spinoza or the Stoics. So this leaves her 'secularized' sense of necessity unsupported. In short, it is hard to see how it can do this job of sustaining meaning and purpose without smuggling back at least something of the wider religious world view which she has rejected.

Nonetheless, although Lloyd's own position is ultimately unsatisfactory, her overall analysis is still revealing. It confirms generally how persistently meaning and purpose seeks new homes and new drivers, even in a disenchanted or secularized world. More substantively, it puts necessity properly on the map as one of those major drivers. It is a valuable reminder that at least some sense of givenness and necessity, as well as its counterpoint of freedom, does play a part in framing meaning and purpose. We seek goals in relation to what is given from beyond as well as what is chosen from within, and Lloyd's discussion has mapped this well.

There is value too in Lloyd's reminder of the pressure to find meaning in the whole and not just the part – a move which Hegel epitomized and took to a kind of logical conclusion (for both metaphysical and aesthetic reasons).[21] Morality and theology will balk at this in its extreme form; yet we do still need some sense of the whole to make sense.

Finally, it demonstrates at least an implicit appeal to reinstate transcendence in our metaphysics. The meaning that presses through notions of fate and necessity begs some wider religious or metaphysical foundations to give some form of transcendent home to it – even though Lloyd herself resists it. That is what this mapping of the persistent sense of objective meaning and purpose reveals even in a world which has rejected this transcendence in so many of its old forms.

---

[20] Lloyd, *Providence Lost*, p. 324.
[21] Cf. Cyril O'Regan, 'Hegel, Theodicy and the Invisibility of Waste', in Francesca Murphy and Philip Ziegler (eds), *The Providence of God* (London: T & T Clark, 2009), pp. 75–108.

Meaning in narrative

A second key driver of meaning and purpose is the structure of narrative itself. We find or make meaning in historical and personal events through our basic disposition to order events in a sequence or pattern. When events are shaped or steered in a certain determinate way, meaning is made and purpose is found. As such, narrative appears to be not just a location of meaning and purpose but also its generator.

Its role in this respect is particularly striking in personal biography. We tell stories to shape and express and create meaning for ourselves, and for our wider communities. This is a near-universal phenomenon. Whether or not it is combined with the intense inwardness and reflexivity of Augustine and Western modernity, whether or not reckoned to be truthful, story-telling abounds. Across time and culture we all tell stories to give ourselves a 'reality' which matters and a purpose to live for. There is something in us all of T. S. Eliot's old man in *Gerontion* who has to create a story of his life, however fantasized, simply to show that his existence has had significance and purpose.

Both MacIntyre and Taylor, amongst others, have done much to identify this sort of significance that narrative has for us. The changing shape of the sequence of events which constitute our life is fundamental to it, says Taylor. Thus:

> The issue of our condition can never be exhausted for us by what we are, because we are always also changing and becoming. ... So the issue for us has to be not only where we are but where we're going ... [and if] we want our lives to have meaning or weight ... this means our whole lives ... if necessary we want the future to 'redeem' the past, *to make it part of a life story which has sense or purpose,* to take it up in a meaningful unity.[22]

In other words, our actual lives may seem fragmentary or unconnected, but they are given meaning and unity by a structure which incorporates them into a narrative shape. In this way we see that the mere sequence of 'events' is just the raw material for meaning and purpose; it is a narrative which *links* events to create both a sense of unity and a teleology which is their real driver.

---

[22] Taylor, *Sources of the Self*, pp. 47, 50–1 (emphasis mine).

The nature of this narrative, however, needs clarification. Narrative, by definition, is a way of linking events, but this can take different forms. Linking can follow a non-linear pattern. Or else it follows a linear, temporal, pattern. So do either of these have a monopoly in generating meaning and purpose?

It appears not. The broad distinctions Gillespie drew between pre-modernity and modernity have already illustrated how meaning and a sense of purpose can emerge from both or either of these. Meaning, as we have seen, can emerge synchronically from non-linear links between cycles or patterns of events, or diachronically by linking a succession of unrepeatable events in a line of development. We know this from ordinary experience, both private and public. For example, even in an era when historical progression predominates, we can still experience just as much meaning and purpose in the synchronic or timeless resonance between (say) a particular piece of music and a declaration of love, as between the linear development which links the proposal of marriage and the date of the wedding the next year. Or we can see as much meaning and purpose in the synchronic resonance between (say) an event in the Arab Spring and the release of the Burmese leader Aung San Suu Kyi, as between each of these and whatever happens next in the linear political development of these countries (in which spring may also turn to winter). That implies at the very least that our successive experience of time is not the only way to generate meaning. It may not even be a sufficient way. Non-linear linking of events can clearly generate meaning alongside linear narrative.

This is reinforced by literary considerations. Douglas Hedley, for example, offers a compelling account of the persistence of non-linear meaning in his book on imagination.[23] Like Gillespie, he notes it has pre-modern origins, in Platonism and Augustine, but he also goes on to chart it in later romanticism and modernity, in Coleridge and in Proust. The essence of it is also nicely articulated by C. S. Lewis in his essay about storytelling. There he describes the way we look for an elusive meaning which linear and successive patterns of events do *not* quite capture: 'we grasp at a state and find only a succession of events in which the state is never quite embodied. ... In life and art both, as

---

[23] Douglas Hedley, *Living Forms of the Imagination* (London: T & T Clark, 2008).

it seems to me, we are always trying to catch in our net of successive moments something that is not successive.'[24]

As Hedley notes, there are critics. Martha Nussbaum, for example, is notoriously wary of this form of finding meaning.[25] It implies for her that meaning is being sought in a contradiction of the very texture of life which makes us human, namely our temporality and its intrinsic sense of successiveness. As such, its implied escape to some sort of transcendent generator of meaning denies who and what we are as human. Yet Nussbaum still appeals to a notion of 'internal' transcendence to drive meaning – and that is an acknowledgement of a need to shape experience with at least *something* beyond ordinary linear succession.

This is borne out in much late-modern deconstruction of linear narrative. Late modernity, as we have seen, is clearly not convinced by simple linear succession, nor an easy developmental narrative. It is driven instead to find new kinds of links in order to generate meaning and purpose – that is part of what 'deconstruction' means. So, as Ricoeur and others have made clear, we have to pay attention to the role of metaphor and differently weighted meaning within narratives in order to receive meaning and purpose from them. This is another way in which the instinct to discover meaning in non-successive patterns of events, as well as linear events, remains strong.

None of this implies we are returning to pre-modernity and a naive notion of meaning just through cyclical events, as if the turn to history has not happened at all. But it does at least suggest that there is no single self-evident notion of narrative shape to drive meaning, and certainly not just a linear shape. As such it keeps pointing us to the underlying dynamic of narrative as something which itself actually generates meaning.

Moreover, it raises a similar question about narrative in general to that raised about necessity. What is its ultimate ground? The very variety of narrative shape begs this question: who or what determines it? To suggest it is determined simply by the given succession of events as they unfold in time is obviously inadequate. The whole point is that we experience meaning

---

[24] C. S. Lewis, 'On Stories', in Lesley Walmsley (ed.), *C.S. Lewis: Essay Collection and Other Short Pieces* (London: HarperCollins, 2000), pp. 491–504.

[25] Cf. discussion in Fergus Kerr, *Immortal Longings: Versions of Transcending Humanity* (London: SPCK, 1997), ch. 1.

through *different* configurations and relations between events. So who or what is configuring them in this way? Presumably much of it is due to the exercise of human will or desire. But is that really sufficient to account for all this persistent variety and extraordinary depth of meaning that different narratives generate? Or are we also driven to posit another transcendent source shaping it for us?

Charles Taylor in *A Secular Age* certainly hints at the latter. For him it is precisely this elusiveness, persistence and depth of meaning conveyed through different kinds of narrative shaping, that is most suggestive of a transcendent source. Thus in the context of an overall account of secularization he tracks many complex, nuanced and multilayered stories and 'social imaginaries' of very different kinds – and then shows that although these stories of meaning display no common form or causal link they do often display common signs of transcendence. That is to say, they convey such a depth of moral, aesthetic, personal meaning that they belie the overall processes of secularization and disenchantment in which they are variously implicated. As such they witness to some form of transcendent meaning and purpose even though their meaning is now often displaced from their traditional home (i.e. theism and the will of a personal God). They are countervailing stories, or 'cross pressures', to straightforward secularization.

Charles Taylor and 'displaced transcendence': Meaning in personal agency, aesthetic experience, moral motivation

This needs further exploration – and for Taylor this is partly done through the sheer comprehensiveness of this mapping of meaning. He covers all the usual landmarks of modernity, and beyond: that is, the emergence of an autonomous (but ultimately problematic) Cartesian self and its quest for meaning through human agency; the influence of neo-Stoicism and its confidence in human capacity to transform society; and the wider shifts from the enchanted world of theism and divine agency, through an intermediate stage of deism, to full-blown humanism. Throughout these narratives he accepts that the 'ontic' component of meaning and morality has, generally, been reduced to an immanent source: that is, viewed on an intra-human basis, rather than based on any transcendent source.[26] Yet precisely within these same familiar stories he also uncovers these cross pressures of displaced transcendence.

What form do these take? They are patterns of meaning which arise from narratives or sub-plots which function synchronically throughout his account, not just sequentially, and which stretch the fabric of a purely immanent and secular frame of meaning which had appeared to be prevailing. One obvious example lies in what he calls the 'post-secular' spiritualities of Europe which lie 'between' the old religious orthodoxies and the apparently prevailing, exclusive, immanent humanism.[27] It is in these sorts of countervailing stories that the human experiences of a displaced but enduring transcendent signifiers are most evident.

These signifiers can also be generically identified. Throughout Taylor's account we constantly encounter the general experiences of responsible personal agency, aesthetic wonder and the sense of an infinite personal moral demand. These generic signifiers are where hints of transcendence are most often apparent. They repay close attention.

Our capacity for personal agency, first, is that obstinate sense that 'we are not just determined … we are active, building, shaping agents'.[28] Of itself this may take us no further than Nussbaum's acknowledgement of our 'natural' human capacity for self-transcendence. Strictly speaking it may not require any further grounding. But it suggests it. It tends to resist a purely social reductionism or biological materialism. For we sometime find so much meaning and mattering in (finite) human action that it begs further grounding to account for it. For example, the intensity of outrage we experience at an act of betrayal is hard to account for solely in terms of a breach of a particular necessary intra-human social contract. Something 'more' has been betrayed by the reality of personal agency. Likewise, the exquisite delight we experience at an act of sacrificial love is not easy to account for solely in terms of the evolutionary necessities of intra-human flourishing. Something 'more' has been honoured and celebrated in the act, and our capacity for personal agency was the foundation for its discovery.

Aesthetic experience has a similar effect. This too generates a sense of intense 'mattering', wonder and value which signifies more than its finite object seems

---

[26] Taylor, *A Secular Age*, p. 256.
[27] Ibid., p. 534.
[28] Ibid., p. 596.

to warrant. As such it again begs metaphysical explanation and a transcendent source. Taylor concedes that non-theistic, purely naturalistic, accounts can always still be offered. He quotes an example of profound aesthetic wonder expressed in terms of a moving but merely naturalist obituary by atheist Richard Dawkins for his friend William Hamilton.[29] But he also insists that even richer and more adequate accounts can be provided if offered 'in the register of religious belief'. Thus: 'there are ... modes of aesthetic experience whose power seems inseparable from their epiphanic nature, that is their revealing something beyond themselves, even beyond nature as we ordinarily know it'.[30]

Then there is moral experience itself. The experience of personal agency or the aesthetic experience which generates such 'infinite' motivation is most powerful precisely and specifically as a sense of *moral* mattering, as moral claim. This is again a transcendent signifier. Here too Taylor acknowledges that purely naturalistic accounts can be offered. Some sort of reductive (Humean) account can always be offered to explain not only the intensity but also the extensity of our moral feelings. There are always some possible 'sentimental' or socio-biological reasons for feeling claimed strongly and widely by our moral commitments. But, again, it is clear that these simply do not convince him. For there is a qualitative difference in what we mean by an instinctive co-operative sentiment towards those with whom we are closely related, and what we mean by this profound (and transcendent) sense of moral duty to, and solidarity with, others.[31]

This difference is rooted in the paradoxical way our moral reaction to particulars also transcends those particulars On the one hand moral meaning, and the motivation which goes with it, is found most acutely in relation to concrete particulars, not just abstract ideas (e.g. one is more likely to die for Jesus, or for a particular political movement, than for 'freedom'). On the other hand this moral meaning found in concrete form does not reduce just to its particular instance. I may feel claimed by someone in particular, but the nature of that claim then seems to extend beyond it as well. It gives meaning to the

---

[29] Ibid., p. 606.

[30] Ibid., p. 607. Taylor offers an example from Bede Griffiths' autobiography, *The Golden String* (London: Fount, 1979), p. 9.

[31] Taylor, *A Secular Age*, p. 608. Here he quotes Ernest Hemmingway in support when he describes 'a feeling of consecration to a duty toward all of the oppressed of the world that would be as difficult and embarrassing to speak about as a religious experience' (from *For Whom the Bell Tolls*, quoted in Piers Brendon, *The Dark Valley* (New York: Knopf, 2000), p. 405.

rest of life too – for even as the value of my own child claims me I also see the same value in other children, at least in principle. Even then its meaning is not exhausted, because the force of the value I experience appears related to something which would be the case even if there were no longer *any* children in view.

In short, this distinctively moral meaning of particular lives or acts seems inexorably to open a window to something ever beyond itself: it keeps pressing the meta-question of 'ultimate' meaning, *le sens du sens*, the very meaning of meaning, the ultimate ground of all value and all meaning.[32] And that is what begs further explanation. It is a powerful transcendent signifier. It is not an attempt to resurrect a decisive moral argument for the existence of God. But it is undoubtedly suggestive.

Taylor is not purporting to write neutrally in this analysis. No one has a view from nowhere and what he finds here in this 'displaced' transcendence may, arguably, be only what he has already assumed through prior religious sympathies. Yet it is not easily dismissed. His approach, after all, is thoroughly disciplined by his much wider methodology. And he is always concerned to frame his discussion within a pluralist and generous hermeneutics of non-religious as well as religious social life and human experience. So this analysis deserves our attention. It is an important part of our mapping of meaning. Narrative, like necessity, is clearly a driver of our sense of meaning and purpose. More than that, it also suggests it is mediating them from something beyond – signified especially in these distinctively human experiences of agency, aesthetics and morality itself.

Moral selves: Simon Critchley, and the spirituality and mystery of the 'infinitely demanding'

Finally, it is worth noting the echoes of this we find even in avowedly non-religious commentators. Simon Critchley, for example, is by his own account a 'faithless' political philosopher.[33] He refuses theism. Yet his account of the

---

[32] Taylor, *A Secular Age*, p. 677. The phrase is from Luc Ferry.
[33] Critchley, *Infinitely Demanding*; his more recent book is *Faith of the Faithless: Experiments in Political Theology* (London: Verso, 2012).

moral self and the infinite nature of the moral demand still reveals similar pressures towards transcendence – of some kind.

Thus right from the outset of his discussion Critchley uses language with an interestingly spiritual quality. He laments the loss of *wonder*. Philosophy from Kant, says Critchley, no longer begins with wonder as it used to, but with disappointment. The disappointment is in our finitude, frailty, failures, in the intellectual life, in religion and in politics. It can lead easily to political nihilisms, of different kinds. It lies behind what he calls a 'motivational deficit' in the sphere of morality. We lack any compelling motivation to be committed to anything, because we no longer see how things matter. We no longer wonder at them in the same way.

At root this is an analysis of the self as well as society, and so for him it is now a central task of philosophy to 'develop a theory of ethical subjectivity'.[34] However, this analysis and programme is not just a forlorn lament. For it goes on to include the recognition that moral motivation has a necessity about it which cannot be allowed to rest unfulfilled. It signifies something essentially normative and, as we shall see, something essentially mysterious as well. And it is here, in his treatment of the necessities and mysteries of moral experience of the ethical subject, that we find interesting echoes of Taylor's analysis.

Critchley reveals this first by expanding his phenomenology of moral experience. He describes how, as a matter of fact, we always encounter our sharpest sense of moral demand in a particular situation. It is the demand of responsibility to another person's well-being and deepest needs, or to the demands of social justice as it relates to particular people. Yet although it arises in a particular situation he echoes the perception we have just noted that its character and force seems to exceed that situation, even to the point of universalizability. Kant, as well as Taylor, would clearly agree.

He also ponders the fact that it presents itself as a demand we cannot wholly meet. It is unfulfillable. This sense is intensified because of its a symmetrical character. From the outside it may look as though it arises out of a reciprocal relationship between myself and an 'other', so that at least we may expect a return. But from the inside the other is not equal and my sense

[34] Critchley, *Infinitely Demanding*, p. 10.

of responsibility is infinite. Levinas, amongst others, is very influential here, as Critchley acknowledges. So on both counts, that is, as universal and infinite, it begs unanswered metaphysical questions.

Critchley is equally interesting when he goes on to map how the ethical self copes, or doesn't, with this experience. Faced with the burden of an unfulfillable demand there could be despair and paralysis. Or there could be the tragic response in which the self achieves its authenticity and satisfactions by heroic failure, ultimately in death. This tragic response also includes an aesthetic dimension, where the attractiveness of the infinite demand remains satisfying even in its projection onto the heroic failure. In psychological terms, this is a form of sublimation; that is, it is the satisfaction of a drive or aspiration by deflecting it from its original goal onto a new one, in this case the goal of heroic tragedy.

The trouble is that this subverts very easily into an egoistic Nietzscherian paradigm. The tragic goal can easily become immoral or amoral, not merely a deflected or limited moral response. So this leads Critchley to propose instead the response of 'humour', another form of sublimation. In this case the frustrated self, potentially torn apart by its failure to reach the moral goal, simply smiles at the lofty aspirations of its own conscience, even ridicules them. In doing this it avoids the despair and depression of impossible aspirations and helps retain hope and commitment; it also avoids enthroning the impossible demand in the distorted or deflected ways of tragedy. But, crucially, the point in doing this is not to deny the demand or its absolute quality. Quite the contrary. It is actually a recognition of its continuing authority. For when the infinite demand is sublimated by humour, it provides a way in which the ethical self can still function – which it 'must' precisely because the infinite moral demand is still exerting a pressure. In other words, Critchley is still endorsing the mystery of an infinite demand, even as he is attempting to cope with it in purely human terms.

Critchley himself still wants to contain all this within an immanent frame. He only toys with metaphysics to ground it, and prefers to turn to psychoanalysis rather than theology to reinterpret Levinas.[35] For him the source of the apparently infinite moral demand is radical human subjectivity,

---

[35] Ibid., p. 67.

not God, and he is trying to offer a phenomenology of moral experience just in these terms. Yet that is precisely why it is so notable that he acknowledges this quality of mystery and absoluteness of the demand. It seems he cannot avoid the sense that this moral demand has at least a 'God-*like*' quality in its sense of an absolute and universal obligation, even though it is conveyed through finite particulars.[36] It is also notable how he is still haunted by images of specifically Judaeo-Christian religion and spirituality, even though rejecting its theology and metaphysics. Like the French atheist philosopher Badiou, Critchley is mesmerized by St Paul's exposition of love precisely as an example of the unconditional nature of this universal demand. Like Løgstrup, a Danish contemporary of Levinas, he also refers to the Sermon on the Mount as a telling example of the 'infinitely demanding'.

To be sure, there is nothing new in moral and political philosophers finding some common ground with theologians in the experience of the ethical demand.[37] But Critchley's particular fascination with its infinite nature remains noteworthy. This is partly just because he has articulated it even within the radical, deconstructive, anarchic, late-modern context of thought with which he is himself generally sympathetic. It is also because of the more subtle affinities with Christian forms of life which he displays. They are good examples of the cross-pressures of the immanent frame, pressing him to adopt religious spiritualities, even if not theology itself.

Thus his appeal to humour has clear affinities with the Christian virtue of humility, even grace. For although he has disavowed the metaphysics of any real God to underlie grace and humility, the way that humour actually functions for him still sounds like a response of a self faced with a reality greater than itself. He co-opts hope in a similar way. Critchleys' self is shaped by a hopeful commitment in spite of the impossible demand and profound disappointments of experience; that too is actually a spiritual disposition, straining at transcendence for both its ground and fulfilment. This appears in even more startling style in his final description of the ultimate source of the moral demand. Here spiritual language again supervenes, with even more significant echoes in Christian theology. Critchley cannot name it 'God', but

---

[36] Ibid., p. 87.
[37] To take just one example, philosophical connections between moral experience and theistic belief are well exploited by Keith Ward, *Ethics and Christian Theology* (London: Allen & Unwin, 1970).

it *is* named 'in the namelessness of a powerless exposure, a vulnerability, a responsive responsibility'.[38] That, of course, has an extraordinary resonance with Christian theology, particularly apophatic theology.

In short, Critchley's phenomenology of a moral self, shaped as it is by a radical commitment to the other and graced with humility and hope, is not only displaying the texture of Christian spirituality, it also hints at Christian theology. These contours of moral experience are gesturing at *God* behind the narratives of our lives and of history, not just at a quality of human 'internal' transcendence. The personal force of the moral demand has begged a metaphysical home in the will of a personal God, not just a phenomenological home in human subjectivity. The humour and the hopefulness have begged an objective divine reality rooted in an historical drama of redemption to ground them, not just a phenomenological reality to display them.

Again, this is not to resurrect a strict argument for the existence of God. It is not a claim that the quandary of moral motivation compels belief in the transcendent. Nor does it require God specifically as the sort of divine agent who authors providence. But in Taylor's words, at least it can 'bring into view certain sites of unease with a [purely] immanent frame'.[39] It sets a context in which the ground, goal and driver of this demand to fulfil (moral) purposes needs explanation. And for some neither a socio-biological or existential explanation alone is adequate. It invites a different and more radical category of transcendence to satisfy such an infinite demand. It suggests God.

Setting the scene for providence

All this maps ways in which transcendent meaning, objective purpose and value, and what drives them, can be tracked through recent intellectual history. Their persistence is remarkable. In the turn to history, then especially in the turn to the self and the processes of disenchantment, they have sometimes been radically challenged. But they have also been consistently re-born. Their transcendence is not wholly lost, just displaced, still sustained by these

[38] Critchley, *Infinitely Demanding*, p. 132.
[39] Taylor, *A Secular Age*, p. 711.

powerful underlying drivers of necessity, narrative and the mystery of moral summons.

Of course, this is a selective account, as all mapping must be. Meaning and purpose could be tracked in more exclusively immanent ways. They could be interpreted through Aristotelian notions of 'internal goods' (i.e. the satisfactions of engaging in any activity in terms of its own nature and ends, whether political activity or contemplation). They could be sought in contemporary utilitarianism, where satisfaction is found in working for external ends (such as relieving suffering). They could be analysed further through notions of natural sympathy, where instincts of attraction towards those closest to us become progressively extended, providing a social structure within which meaning and purpose can develop – whether through Stoic ideas of *oikeiosis* or contemporary accounts from socio-biology.[40] All these are features of human thought and experience which generate a teleology which would *not* require any transcendent source or driver. They remind us that a reductionist approach is always be possible, and the sense of objective purpose can always be subjectively and immanently contained. Value, virtue and a sense of purpose, can and do function at many levels without strictly requiring God.[41]

Nonetheless, this mapping has shown that such purely immanent accounts do not easily satisfy. They will always have to reckon with this other story we have tracked: that persistent sense of purpose which seems to lie beyond human subjectivity and temporality, as well as within it; a purpose located through history, yet not always grasped in a linear way; a meaning experienced in human autonomy but shaped by necessities beyond us as well. Above all, they will have to account for this strange pressure of the 'God-like' imperative of absolute and infinite moral demand which drives this it.

So this pressure remains, incontrovertibly, as part of the map which cannot be ignored. And as such it clearly sets a context for divine providence. Any context in which objective purpose can continue to be found, as well as lost, shows why theism will always find resonance, as well as resistance, when it

---

[40] For a useful recent account of *oikeosis* see Christopher Brooke, 'Grotius, Stoicism and "Oikeiosis"', *Grotiana*, 29 (2008), pp. 25–50.

[41] For an extended essay which explores how value and purpose can function without God, see Erik J. Wielenberg, *Value and Virtue in a Godless Universe* (Cambridge: Cambridge University Press, 2005).

tries to speak of providence; it helps demonstrate why theology has found providence to be 'necessary' as well as impossible.

To be sure, a credible doctrine will need more than this to re-establish itself. There are major issues of conceptual, empirical and moral credibility it always has to face, as later chapters acknowledge. But this map of the sheer persistence of a transcendent purpose does at least help lend weight to it.

2

Loss, Love, Recovery: A Literary Story

A pressure to believe some sense of objective purpose haunts Western thought, with or without a definite theistic frame. That is what the mapping of the previous chapter has helped demonstrate. This sets a context for what follows. It offers encouragement for exploring it further specifically in theism – where, of course, it has always been more intentionally shaped and promulgated. For with theism, as Stephen Clark says, 'we *have* to include in our scenario the thought that 'God is working His purpose out'.[1]

But not yet. The mapping, after all, was hardly monochrome. It included much which counted against a transcendent teleology, as well as for it. Its backdrop was always a loss of purpose, even if its overall narrative showed its persistence as well. So it is important to be sure we do not gloss lightly this contradictory part of the context, before stepping into theistic assumptions. We should test this sense of purpose further.

What has just been charted in the ebb and flow of intellectual history was one way of doing this. The notion of purpose has been tested against a disenchanted backdrop, and found resilient. When Aristotelian and Christian teleology was supposedly expelled by the Enlightenment, a sense of displaced transcendence and objective purpose has persisted. But there is another way to test its resilience. We could review how it fares in more immediate textures of experience – especially in experience which appears to contradict it.

The way I want to do this will now be to review it in literature, especially the novel. This, it seems to me, will test it much more effectively than rational analysis alone. A novel can convey the meaning of our experience in embodied form, through narrative and character. It *displays* a scenario, rather than just

---

[1] Stephen Clark, *God's World and the Great Awakening* (Oxford: Clarendon Press, 1991), p. 187 (emphasis mine).

arguing it, and this offers advantages.² It can offer the overall sensibility and texture of a world view, not just an abstract account of its metaphysics. This, in my view, will do a scenario more justice.³

Accordingly, I will concentrate on two novelists. Both write reflectively, penetratingly, and with clear-eyed honesty and openness to experience. Both also write specifically as agnostics or atheists in their quest for meaning, so they will test a sense of purpose thoroughly.

The first is Thomas Hardy, writing mostly in the late nineteenth century. Hardy represents a critical distance from our own context, as well as some similarities. It was a world in which science and rationality had disenchanted the world and faith was receding, but also a world in which rationality itself had not yet been subject to the same degree of disenchantment that we have known. This distance is valuable. As fish in water cannot understand wetness we may not understand best what we are most immediately immersed in; so it helps to step back into this related but distinct world. The second, Julian Barnes, is a writer much more directly of our own times. He can help convey the scenario right from within where we stand. For he describes the experience of a world in which the disenchantment has become even more radicalized and internalized.

Both writers therefore offer this good test. They clearly demonstrate an overall experience of the world in which God and purpose seem absent. Yet what I will suggest is that, against expectation, they also show a sense of purpose persisting. In spite of their professed scepticism, they demonstrate its presence. Even as they describe its impossibility, they actually bear ironic

---

² 'Scenario' (Clark's phrase) is a good word here. It evokes a sense of the wider scenery of the world, its external landscape, not just the inner landscape of our souls. It assumes a sort of critical realism, therefore, inviting us to think we can access at least something of the 'real' world through any honestly recorded experience. This begs the question whether any such critical realism is in fact still possible. Can it still make sense even to gesture at any 'objective' reality? As noted in Chapter 1, recent trends are wary of dualism between subject and object. We cannot distinguish easily between what is within us and beyond us. Yet the fact that it is hard to disentangle subject and object should not lead us to suppose there is no reality external to us. It is pure obfuscation to refuse to imagine any reality external to us simply on the grounds that our grasp of it is always a subjective act. External reality is too basic to our common sense to deny outright. In any case, in the end few do really deny it: the familiar but poorly expressed post-structuralist claim that 'there is nothing outside the text' is a good case in point. It sounds as if the world consists only of language, whereas it only really means that we cannot disentangle the world from our language: that is, 'nothing in reality stands alone' (Terry Eagleton, *The English Novel*, Oxford: Blackwell, 2005, p. 201). That's true enough. But it doesn't mean there is nothing 'there' to explore through language.
³ As such this appeal to literature is intended to add 'thickness' to the way reality is displayed and experienced, not just to illustrate a viewpoint. In this way it avoids (I hope) the sort of strictures

witness to its necessity. That at least is how I shall read the world they describe in their work.

It should be clear this is not meant as a reading of their own personal beliefs – it is a literary reading not an attempt at biography. But precisely as such, if it is a fair reading, it will be all the more interesting. It will describe the sensibility of an overall world view, not just an individual state of mind. In this way it will show how a persistence sense of purpose is indeed displayed right at the heart of its apparent absence.

Hardy's difficult world

A world view embracing evolution

So – what was Hardy's world? Its most immediate texture, especially in his later novels, is undoubtedly pessimistic and tragic. The pessimism derives directly from an overall perception that the universe is shaped by impersonal laws indifferent to human life. The disasters which befall his characters are not justly ordered to some purpose, any more than the fleeting joys and happinesses. The tragedy is that this objective meaninglessness of the universe renders even our own actions meaningless.[4] This is implicit in the plots which unfold. It is also often made explicit by the narrator. So we are clearly told that 'revelling in the general situation grows less and less possible as we uncover the defects of natural laws and see the quandary that man is in by their operation';[5] nature is not purposeful in any anthropocentric sense, and all notion of 'nature's holy plan' is dismissed with sarcasm.[6]

As Gillian Beer points out, this is indeed radical disenchantment. At least for George Eliot the fixed laws of nature provided some sort of basis for a moral

---

sometimes offered to critique the use of arts in theology. Cf. Ben Quash: 'Scholarship in the arena of theology and the arts is frequently shallow because ... it is prone to the deployment of examples from the arts only when they are deemed useful for the illustration of a preconceived theological viewpoint' (*Found Theology: History, Imagination and the Holy Spirit*, London: Bloomsbury, 2013), p. xvi.

[4] Cf. Stefan Horlacher's view of Jude in 'Jude the Obscure: From a Metaphysics of Presence to the Blessings of Absence,' *Journal of Men, Masculinities and Spirituality*, 1.2 (2007), pp. 116–36. The failure to create meaning even by our own actions is an important part of tragedy.

[5] Thomas Hardy, *The Return of the Native* (Harmondsworth: Penguin Classics, 1985), p. 255.

[6] Thomas Hardy, *Tess of the D'Urbevilles* (Oxford: Oxford World's Classics, 1998), p. 28.

universe, even if it is godless. Or for Emile Zola, there is at least the fecundity of nature to compensate for its death and destruction.[7] But for Hardy neither the fixity nor the fecundity is benign or positively purposeful. They are simply part of that which is over against human control, and which is just as liable to frustrate or destroy us as to provide for us. Nature's laws, says Jude in Hardy's last and most tragic novel, seemed to promise joy but 'now Fate has given us this stab in the back for being such fools as to take Nature at her word'.[8]

The background for this disenchantment is not hard to trace. Others have speculated on biographical reasons, but so far as the general context of thought is concerned it is easy to see what provided the framework. Schopenhauer's scepticism almost certainly had some effect. Even more telling was Darwin. His evolutionary theory was clearly an influence in both its original form as natural science and in its extension to cultural theory. Darwin, as we know, found the processes of the world to be, precisely, random and impersonal; a system existing without specific thought for human well-being.

In fact Hardy seems to have made this evolutionary theory serve an even bleaker world view than Darwin himself. For Darwin the vastness of the timescale beyond human existence was a positive source of wonder. But for Hardy the immensity often just intensified the frustration of our own human finitude and thwarted aspirations. For Darwin the mechanisms of randomness and survival were at least partly beneficial, enabling overall progression to higher and fitter forms of life. But for Hardy it was almost all cruel. The fittest may conquer and survive, but not the deserving or best, not Tess. Overall Darwin's narrative of the world actually retains quite strong vestiges of overall purpose and intention – as Beer says, he uses a language 'thick with assumptions of intention and agency' even in arguments that seem to deny those very assumptions.[9] But in Hardy, especially when we reach *Jude*, there are moments when there appears to be no hope or meaning in *any* sort of purpose. 'Rightly seen' the world is but a first cause 'working as a somnambulist, not reflectively like a sage'. All we have around us is just 'senseless circumstance'.[10] All creation is reduced just to groaning – and unlike the Pauline metaphor

---

[7] Gillian Beer, *Darwin's Plots: Evolutionary Narrative in Darwin, George Eliot and Nineteenth-Century Fiction* (Cambridge: Cambridge University Press, 2000), p. 223.

[8] Thomas Hardy, *Jude the Obscure* (Harmondsworth: Penguin Classics, 1985), p. 413.

[9] Beer, *Darwin's Plots*, p. xii.

[10] Hardy, *Jude*, p. 417.

this is groaning without purpose, without redemption and even without any hope of solace. It is a world where different interests, desires and patterns of behaviour inevitably and senselessly conflict, so that there is always damage being done, even to the well intentioned – the archetypal conditions of tragedy written deep into its very structures. It is, in Edwin Muir's terms, 'a difficult land' where 'things miscarry, whether we care or do not care enough' – and unlike Muir that is all; there is no 'other side of time' to hint at other hopes.[11]

The only element of evolution which Hardy seems to find positive is the sheer abundance of life which is required for its selections, and at times he does seem to revel in the springtime burst of life on Egdon Heath, just as he revels in the diversity and vitality of human life and human passions – something we shall return to later. Yet ultimately even these celebrations of life still become material for poignancy and pessimism. They create an even greater sense of tragedy when that diversity of life is crushed by the very same processes which generated it. So while tragedy may not be the only perspective Hardy has on natural abundance and human joy, it is certainly a dominant one. As such, the overall texture of Hardy's world view appears to remain, irredeemably, a scenario of radical godlessness and purposelessness; a world in which human meaning appears only temporary, self-created, doomed to futility and extinction.

Cracks in the picture: Subverting evolution?

But now a closer look. Is that really all Hardy conveys? In fact we find Hardy's world rather less monochrome, and more paradoxical, than sometimes thought. Its bleakness is, occasionally, punctuated by flashes of a rather different light – both existentially and conceptually.

For a start, what we find in Hardy's world is a very powerful and persistent perception of individual *mattering*. He consistently conveys a sense of extraordinary value in individual and particular being. Hardy's world is a place of particular things and people which compel our attention and generate a sense of value, even when they have been cast aside by circumstance, or simply the passage of time. Even the cattle long since past are given abiding value in Tess's milking shed. Most of all, the human characters are almost all

---

[11] Edwin Muir, 'The Difficult Land', *Selected Poems* (London: Faber & Faber, 1965), p. 82.

painted with profound sympathy. They are tracked through their life by their
narrator with something approaching devotion. Both the inner texture of their
particular experiences, and their outward behaviour and destiny, are shown to
matter. This is not diminished in the least by a clear-eyed view of their flaws.
Nor, crucially, does it cease when they seem to have been reduced to pawns in
the hand of blind fate.

This is significant because it implicitly challenges aspects of a merely
evolutionary world view. For it is not just the successful and the survivors who
command this interest and sympathy. Tess herself is not the survivor – but she
is nonetheless a heroine. Likewise Henchard in *The Mayor of Casterbridge*. He
is no success. He is both profoundly flawed and a victim of circumstance. Yet
he still evokes huge sympathy, even though he dies without any further will
to live and without any notable legacy.[12] Hardy expresses this unique kind of
individual mattering structurally by confining the plots of these novels to a
single life span. As Gillian Beer points out, the stories begin and end with the
life of a central character. The plot honours individuals by ending with their
death, unlike Eliot and Dickens who sometimes include their death within the
plot.[13]

This presents an interesting paradox. It flies in the face of the underlying
logic of evolution which has otherwise shaped Hardy. In purely evolutionary
biological terms an individual organism has *no* particular value in itself,
because it does not itself evolve in its own life cycle. Only if it happens to
generate or procreate an offspring which is better fitted for survival does it
temporarily contribute to the evolutionary process. After that it ceases to have
any significance itself. In any case, the plenitude of nature throws out millions
of these procreations which do not even get selected for this temporary value.
They serve no particular purpose at all. This can also be true of whole species.
They too can die out without further significance, as Darwin realized when
he discovered lost life forms of the past. Yet all that is precisely what Hardy's
perception of individual value paradoxically resists.

Hardy's protest against the moral logic of evolution is also implicit in his
critique of human society, whenever he sees this too being ordered in an
evolutionary way. Particular human experience, its hopes and deepest desires

---

[12] Thomas Hardy, *The Mayor of Casterbridge* (Harmondsworth: Penguin Classics, 1997).
[13] Beer, *Darwin's Plots*, p. 223.

(notably women's as well as men's), has value which should not be crushed by social convention for some supposed common good – just as it should not be frustrated by natural fate for the sake of some supposed evolutionary 'progress'. So when Jude and Sue suffer persecution for their relationship there is outrage to be felt against human society, as well as a protest against nature when they suffer a stillbirth.

In short, for all his evolutionary backdrop and overall pessimism, it seems Hardy cannot wholly accept it. His vision of life sees and conveys meaning and value in particularity which evolutionary theory does not itself contain. Things and people do not simply mediate a passing instrumental value to some supposed fitter future or greater good. Nor are they just the detritus of a wasteful blind process. Instead, they matter in themselves. The leading question that this paradox of human mattering then leaves unanswered is this: since evolution itself cannot generate this value, *what or who does?* It is a recurring question that the mysteries of our moral sense always put to reductionist world views. At root it is the same sort of question that we saw haunting the more contemporary atheism of Critchley.[14]

A reductionist view is also challenged by other features of Hardy's vision. I have already mentioned his revelling in natural plenitude. Even more significant, Hardy revels in the rich diversity and extraordinary vitality of specific human joys, especially of sense experience. Nature (and society) may have the ubiquitous capacity to crush joy, but it still bubbles up irrepressibly. So for example, the narrator has Tess and Clare driving 'though the gloom', yet still overcome by 'the appetite for joy which pervades all creation … that tremendous force which sways humanity to its purpose'.[15] Such happiness may be tenuous and short-lived, but here at least it is possible – and even seems in some sense to be 'intended'.

This joy and exuberance within life is often expressed in dance, with all the intrinsic optimism about change and renewal that dance conveys.[16] Dance is a recurring feature, not only in the earlier and more optimistic *Under the Greenwood Tree* but also, for example, in *Tess*. It ends there in a kind of disintegration, but that does not erase the fact that it happened. In other

---

[14] See pp. 32–6 above.
[15] Hardy, *Tess*, p. 191.
[16] Cf. Simon Gatrell, *Thomas Hardy and the Proper Study of Mankind* (London: Macmillan, 1993), ch. 2.

words, there is something within the social and 'natural' experience of his characters which keeps generating (or reflecting) an ever present *possibility* of joy – even though it may actually end in tears. As already suggested, this possibility heightens the tragedy when the joy is denied, yet its very possibility still remains a significant presence in the text. Like land over the horizon of the sea, it makes a presence felt, even in its absence.

In this context the sad endings of the novels should not necessarily be seen as the last word. The texture of the narrative as a whole has been too rich and multilayered for that. It suggests that Hardy finds such possibilities of joy significant, even when they are unfulfilled. Gillian Beer puts it like this:

> We always sustain until the last moment a passionate sense of possible happiness: he sustains hope ... by multiple perspectives. And the drive of his plots is so crushing precisely because of the full sense of life elated in us by the range of sense perceptions which are evoked through his writing. ... Looking back on a novel by Hardy many readers are afflicted and aghast. But he is also one of the most popular and widely read of writers: we enter his works not only to be chagrined and thwarted, but also sustained by the moment-by-moment plenitude of experience offered us. Traumatised by conclusion, the reader in retrospect almost forgets the bounty of text. Forgetting and having are both crucial in Hardy.[17]

In other words, a wholly pared-down world of pure randomness and purposeless is not quite all there is for him. Something more positive appears, inescapably there, even when the plot appears to close it down.

Another way in which Hardy – or at least one of Hardy's voices – finds himself subverting Darwinism is in his latent idealism. This is not immediately apparent. *Prima facie* Hardy is no idealist. He deals in empirical realism and particularism. He pays close attention to what is actually visible and evident to the senses in particular times and places. Nature proceeds in its changes and chances, and impinges on human life, only as we observe it happening in particular cases. Any attempt to universalize, to interpret these happening according to an intended overarching idea or 'order', especially one which has human interests at heart, is misguided, only a 'whimsical fancy'.[18] This is why particular and local space and time is, for the most part, the only real place

---

[17] Beer, *Darwin's Plots*, p. 231.
[18] Hardy, *Tess*, p. 91.

of significance for Hardy. Egdon Heath in *The Return of the Native* is a good example of this. It functions to delimit an area of life and concern. So the grand theatre of the world as a whole, the Tolstoyan epic scale of events set on a wide stage and interpreted through some wider philosophy of history, is not for Hardy. He tries to avoid the fusion of big events and big ideas.

Yet in fact Hardy's world does not reduce to particulars quite so easily. The intense gaze which he devotes to particular realities sometimes also seems to yield a transcendent meaning. Thus, for example, in spite of its particularity and its eventfulness, Egdon Heath also seems timeless, changeless, limitless, almost an eternal reality. It is a 'vast tract of unenclosed wild' which 'hardly heeded change', and on which 'there was no absolute hour of day'.[19] This is not a realistic view of what was, empirically, just a relatively small and transient area of heathland. Instead it breathes an underlying idealism in which a sense of transcendence and absoluteness supervenes. Like Edward Thomas's *Adlestrop* where a single blackbird's song in one place contains all song in all places, this 'unenclosed' wild hints at a haunting sense of the universal in the particular, the eternal in the temporal – something which no programme of empiricism can ever quite obliterate. Within a world view of philosophical idealism or romanticism such universalism would be a natural and ready handmaid. But even in this more rigorous world of empiricism and realism it still appears. Like wild flowers in a cultivated field, it still breaks surface.

Latent idealism and universalism is also suggested in Hardy's poetry.[20] His wartime poem of 1915 'In Time of "The Breaking of Nations"' is a spare simple vision of just a ploughman and two lovers passing by. But it is not 'just' this. In these unremarkable local figures Hardy senses something strangely transcendent, of more significance even than the backdrop of the global war behind them. He sees something which will '... go onward the same/ Though Dynasties pass ... War's annals will could into night/ere their story die'. Even where the narrative of a poem ends by destroying such simple images, the power in the vision of what went before persists and somehow outranks the ending. So in his poetry as in his novels the meaning is not just in the plot – it also transcends plot.

---

[19] Hardy, *Return of the Native*, pp. 53, 161, 186.
[20] James Gibson (ed.), *Thomas Hardy: The Complete Poems* (New York: Palgrave, 2001). See especially 500; 441; 119.

This is also evident in 'During Wind and Rain'. The poem charts the narrative of ordinary, yet extraordinary, domestic lives, in a sequence of simple images of singing and breakfasting, bringing up children and tending gardens. Each of these images is then briefly and savagely undermined at the end of each stanza, so that change and decay seem to have the last word. But in fact the preceding images have been so potent that what abides most in the mind is the value of what is lost, not the losing of it. So – could it be that it is not lost after all? Could there be, in the final words of 'The Darkling Thrush', 'some blessed Hope' after all? In other words, there are particular visions of 'eternal' value throughout his poetry which function like the episodes of joy in his novels. They evoke transcendent meaning which belies the apparent shape of the story being told. As one commentator puts it, 'the "yes" they are saying to life transcends the grinding inevitabilities [of change and destruction]'.[21]

All this – the persistent sense of human mattering, the possibility of joy, the hints of a universalism and transcendence – presents a brave vision of meaning in a hostile or indifferent universe. But is it any more than that? Does it do any more than add poignancy? Does it signify anything other than the human attempt to *create* meaning and purpose, rather than the discovery of some actual transcendent purpose?

The most usual answer may still seem to be no. We still have to accept that both narrator and main characters repeatedly and explicitly tell us that nature is blind. We also have to accept that structurally, the plots reinforce this. They increasingly embody the tragic consequences of such a world, especially if we look to their endings. Our fleeting joys and aspirations may try to subvert our endings, but the objective finality of structure is hard to gainsay for ever. However long we wait for another end, nobody and nothing will ultimately overrule this world to good purpose and to our benefit. As the young Jude realized early on in his life after one such waiting, such hope is always ultimately crushed: 'nobody did come because nobody does'. To think otherwise remains simply 'a gigantic error'.[22] For even if something does happen to happen, it doesn't happen intentionally *for me*: the agencies are the world are simply indifferent to us. One of Hardy's later poems expresses it graphically like this: 'A car comes up, with lamps full-glare/ That flash upon a tree/ It has nothing

[21] Tom Paulin, *Thomas Hardy: The Poetry of Perception* (London: Macmillan, 1975), p. 210.
[22] Hardy, *Jude*, p. 72.

to do with me/ And whangs along in a world of its own/ Leaving a blacker air; /And mute by the gate I stand again alone/ And nobody pulls up there.'[23] It is like Beckett's *Waiting for Godot*: it is a *non*-event of providence. And these powerful negatives images may well seem to prevail.

Yet even in these bleakest assertions of objective meaningless, there remains this paradox. Even the 'non-events' are recorded as if they are significant. So why are they even recorded? Above all, who is this narrator who records them? Perhaps the 'gigantic error' is not so much the belief that somebody will come and something will happen, but in mistaking this rhetoric of negativity for the only voice. Perhaps there are multiple voices, and more than one viewpoint being narrated. These include the immediate experience of absence, but they also include some perception of presence and significance.

In short, perhaps we do not have to choose or close between options after all. Subjective and objective purpose are both still, just, possibilities. There *may* after all be some 'spinner of the years' lying behind events, non-events and even disastrous events – if only an impersonal fate.[24] And this is surely a particularly significant admission when it is being wrung out of the heart of a scenario which, mostly, denies it outright.

Which Hardy? Whose viewpoint?

This sense of different narrative viewpoints is important. Hardy comes at the end of the realistic tradition of novel writing with its god-like omniscient narrator, and he is clearly no longer entirely bound by it. Instead, he is offering this different stance in which the narrator deliberately adopts a variety of standpoints and perspectives. As more than one commentator has pointed out, Hardy likes to use the optative mood in making his comments: 'why did nobody see this or do that...' and 'had somebody or something occurred then...' and so on. These hypotheticals hint at a contingency and a freedom of things to be otherwise, even as they interlock with the blind necessities of natural law. They are a way of adopting different perspectives, different angles

[23] Gibson (ed.), *Hardy: Complete Poems*, p. 715.
[24] A phrase from Hardy's poem on the sinking of the Titanic, 'The Convergence of the Twain': Gibson (ed.), *Hardy: Complete Poems*, p. 248. I have briefly signalled this ambivalent reading of Hardy in an earlier article: Vernon White, 'Providence, irony and belief: Thomas Hardy – and an improbable comparison with Karl Barth', *Theology*, CXIII (2010), pp. 357–65.

to his 'camera lens'. Hence Eagleton, trying to describe Hardy's overall view of
humanity in relation to nature, finds a complex mood to his viewing:

> [Hardy's god-like stance] ... is less of a scientific doctrine than an imaginative
> hypothesis. What would all this frenetic human striving look like from the
> lofty vantage-point of Mount Olympus? Or, indeed, from the viewpoint of
> the evolutionary process as a whole? ... What would it feel like to view your
> own life in this fatalistic light?' ... Sometimes his camera is angled so that a
> typical Hardy tale would begin: If you had been on this road at such-and-
> such a time you would have seen. ...[25]

Hardy is not just trying out these different perspectives *qua* narrator. He also
allows his characters to ponder alternative viewpoints in conversation with
the narrator. A good example is a discussion in *The Mayor of Casterbridge*,
specifically about the notion of providence, where Hardy allows his characters
both traditional prevailing views and more radical, sceptical views. This does
not mean that the narrator is just trying to persuade his characters to change
from one to the other. In a fascinating, oscillating, sequence of dialogue and
comment – which embraces fate, freedom and providence – I sense no one
dominating authorial voice pronouncing *the* proper outcome.[26]

   Thus we hear Lucetta secularizing providence as a neutral fate; Elizabeth Jane
assuming a more traditional personal God at work; and a narrator preferring
a notion of impersonal destiny. But there is no magisterial voice arbitrating
here, nor any structural necessity to choose. True, Henchard himself starts
with a strong view of the supernatural which then dies in him as time and
circumstance bite. As a narrator says, 'the emotional conviction that he was
in Somebody's hands began to die out in Henchard', and we are told that the
belief had been the mere superstition and emotion of 'an unintellectual' man.
But then this is challenged by the persistence of (another?) narrator who
continues to use the language of fate and destiny: it is a 'fate' which determines
that Henchard is thwarted, as if this is some intention or agency at work. In the
end, when Elizabeth watches her mother dying and asks the inevitable aching
question 'why things around her had taken the shape they wore', no narrator
offers any answer at all. The many voices are all silent. Who then is the real

---

[25] Eagleton, *The English Novel*, pp. 196, 199.
[26] Hardy, *The Mayor of Casterbridge*.

Hardy? This is surely more like an undecided or unsettling world view than a monocrome or didactic one. It is, in that sense, an ironic view.

There is irony too in Hardy's accounts of the interconnectedness of things. There is an ambivalence about it. On the one hand the rational voice asserts that there is nothing but natural laws of necessity and randomness to create human experience. Thus 'history is rather a stream than a tree. There is nothing organic in its shape, nothing systematic its development.'[27] On the other hand this does not simply settle all questions of meaning when processes collide and events occur. The theme of the great web of reality, beloved by Eliot and other Victorians, remains present and problematic for Hardy, for things clearly do interconnect and when they do they matter: 'the human race [is] one great network or tissue which quivers in every part, like a spider's web when touched'.[28] In his novels something of this is frequently expressed when small things like a lost letter, missed appointment or unconscious gesture can trigger major consequences. Such events are pregnant with meaning within the narrative flow, even if one voice has dismissed them as mere chance.

As with the discussion of providence, this leaves us with different perspectives, or just silence, but certainly no single definitive authorial conclusion. The notion of 'the spinner of the years' as an impersonal 'immanent will' flowing through this web of events is perhaps the nearest we get to a resolution, but that hardly resolves the complexity and ambiguity of all that he describes in his world.[29]

Hardy's world, then, clearly has different voices and different perspectives. Although, overall, it is a godless world without objective purpose, its disenchantment is not wholesale. It is full of cracks for other meaning to enter. These cracks are not left open just as a sop to other sensibilities or because he was unwilling to offend. Hardy did not lack integrity or moral courage to write as he truly saw, even if that meant describing a purposeless world which failed to provide solace – he was duly chastised by Victorian critics for just that.[30] But in fact what he saw was not 'just that'; the full texture of life he experienced,

---

[27] From Florence Hardy, *The Early Life of Thomas Hardy* (London: Macmillan, 1928), pp. 219ff.

[28] *Diary* entry 4 March 1886, quoted in Beer, *Darwin's Plots*, p. 157.

[29] This seems clearest in his play *The Dynasts*.

[30] Although different drafts suggest he sometimes revised his writing, he was always risking and receiving opprobrium: even when *Jude* provoked major controversy, marking the end of his novel writing, Hardy merely moved on to a new form of writing, not necessarily a new vision of reality cf. Eagleton's discussion in *The English Novel*.

even against the backdrop of tough-minded evolutionary theory, kept resisting total reductionism. It breathes value, purpose, even a hint of agencies at work, which have to be included in some way, alongside their negation. That is what required these different ways of narrating our life, however ambiguous, opaque, or incompatible.

Interestingly, in this respect Hardy proves close to Darwin again. For even Darwin's *Origin of Species* is at times an ironic narrative of life, as much as a definitive theory.[31] It is a narrative which includes different perspectives. As already noted, it often finds itself using language of agency and intention alongside assumptions of purely impersonal processes.[32] Moreover, like Hardy, Darwin does not seem to be conceding this ambiguity just as some fading vestige of his own personal background; it is intrinsic to 'reality itself' (i.e. evolutionary theory).[33]

This is now increasingly accepted as a characteristic of all scientific theory and discourse, not just as some primitive flaw in Darwinism. As Stephen Prickett says, we no longer expect our scientific paradigms to be 'unambiguous and unironic'.[34] Even mathematics has this kind of irony at its heart, if Godel's incompleteness theorem is accepted. It is begging for 'something more', even if it cannot define it.[35] None of this means, of course, that Hardy himself wrote out of particular scientific sophistication. But it is a further illustration of the ironic texture of reality that Hardy's world conveys.

---

[31] See, for example, Beer, *Darwin's Plots*, and Stephen Prickett, *Narrative, Religion and Science: Fundamentalism versus Irony 1700–1999* (Cambridge: Cambridge University Press, 2002).

[32] To be sure, Darwin is aware of this and comments on it himself as if it can be discounted. He says metaphorical expressions are 'almost necessary ... so it is difficult to avoid personifying the word Nature ... but I mean by Nature only the aggregate action and product of many natural laws and by laws the sequence of events as ascertained by us' (quoted in Beer, *Darwin's Plots*, p. 63). Nonetheless, the ambiguity is revealing. In his fascinating study of narrative and science, Stephen Prickett makes just this point: 'far from being superficial they [that is, Darwin's ambiguities] seem to be endemic to the whole argument, so that what looked like a minor linguistic problem has turned into something much more deep rooted and central to the whole theory', Prickett, *Narrative, Religion and Science*, p. 30.

[33] Thus Beer, *Darwin's Plots*, pp. 7–8: 'Evolutionary theory is a form of imaginative itself. ... It has been imaginatively powerful precisely because all its indications do not point one way. It is rich in contradictory elements which can serve as a metaphorical basis for more than one reading of experience.'

[34] Prickett, *Narrative, Religion and Science*, p. 30. Following Polanyi's *Personal Knowledge* and Kuhn's *Structure of Scientific Revolutions*, and notwithstanding their subsequent critics, it is widely agreed that science offers different narratives of this world rather than definitive theories.

[35] Cf. Prickett, *Narrative, Religion and Science*, pp. 82–3, citing Roger Penrose, *Times Higher Education Supplement*, 3 April 1998. If no theorem can prove itself to be self sufficient, it requires some further truth beyond itself: its very incompleteness points to 'something more'.

Irony, realism and honesty

To ascribe this sort of irony to Hardy (and Darwin) is not to project back onto them the more reductionist irony from the fashionable rhetoric of some postmodern definitions. That sort of irony refers to the ambiguities or gaps in meaning between one linguistic formulation and another: that is, an ironic gap *within* language, rather than the gap *between* language and reality itself. Richard Rorty and others who speak as if there is nothing outside the text may use the term in this way as part of the flight from realism and, ultimately, truth itself. But the scientific community would hardly subscribe to that. Nor would somebody like Prickett. And neither do I when ascribing it to Hardy.[36] Instead, I am using irony here in the more traditional sense which critical realism allows: that is, as a way of referring to the gaps and ambiguities between language and reality, between words and 'truth'. I see Hardy, like science, engaging with the ambiguities of reality, not just of texts or ideas.

This irony of critical realism uses uncertainty more openly and positively than a complete flight from realism allows. On the one hand, in our engagement with reality, this irony accepts there will be a limiting and distorting connection between subjective and objective. It assumes that, to some degree, we are bound to be subsuming the external world to ourselves, projecting ourselves into the world, 'bending' the world into our own anthropomorphic and anthropocentric shape (a form of Ruskin's pathetic fallacy). In that sense we must admit that we may sometimes be seeing the world as 'thick with intention and agency' whether or not that agency is really there in the cracks we encounter. But on the other hand the uncertainty opened up by this irony also allows the possibility of the opposite: that is, it means we cannot necessarily deny that what we see through these cracks may be really there (any more than we can necessarily affirm it), so it allows that those intimations of agency and intention *could* be a reflection of reality, not just a projection. Irony in this sense is therefore, at root, simply an aspect of fundamental honesty. It is a genuine openness to reality, a determination to keep *all* possibilities alive.

That is exactly what I see in Hardy. It is well expressed in a passage from *Tess*, where she is placed in just this complex sort of relation to a world which

---

[36] I have already signalled that such radical retreat into language and text is misleading: see p. 40 note 2 above.

is both around her and within her. Tess is out walking, and thinking. The narrator describes the experience:

> On these lonely hills and dales her quiescent glide was of a piece with the element she moved in. Her flexuous and stealthy figure became an integral part of the scene. At times her whimsical fancy would intensify natural processes around her till they seemed a part of her own story. Rather they became part of it; for the world is only a psychological phenomenon, and what they seemed they were. The midnight airs and gusts ... were formulae of bitter reproach. A wet day was the expression of irremediable grief at her weakness in the mind of some vague being ...[37]

Here, certainly, is a testimony to subjectivity, the power of the self to project itself into everything around it and mould it into her own shape. It is an experience of the natural world moulded into a personified shape by the anthropocentric observer in the very process of describing the experience. That is why the world appears 'only a psychological phenomenon'. But here too is this more nuanced ironic vision, because we are also told it is Tess's 'whimsical fancy' which was grasping it like this and which made it 'what it seemed' to her. Those telling phrases cut both ways. For they make every judgement unreliable, and leave the narrator and reader to see things in any number of other ways as well.[38] As such it appears to be the opaqueness of reality itself which is generating an uncertainty here, as well as Tess's own subjectivity. And that in turn leaves us always entitled to see more, not less in the mysteries of experience which present themselves.

Such irony is surely an important ingredient in exploring the world. As Prickett points out, it constitutes a challenge to all fundamentalisms, whether of religion or science. Yet it also challenges pure constructivism – precisely because it arises from this engagement with a real world beyond ourselves. It can be found in such disparate sources as Kiekegaard and, as noted, contemporary science.[39] And what it helps uncover is just what we suspected: if we enter the disenchanted modern world with the sort of honest and ironic gaze that Hardy demonstrates, we find we cannot entirely eliminate purposiveness

---

[37] Hardy, *Tess*, p. 91.
[38] They also leave Tess herself to have different perspectives at different times. So, for example, Tess can see at times it is *not* simply the 'God of her childhood' that she senses, even though 'she could not comprehend [it] as any other'. Hardy, *Tess*, p. 91.
[39] Cf. the discussion in Prickett, *Narrative, Science and Religion*, pp. 256ff.

after all. Although it is a world overwhelmingly experienced as godless and purposeless, real attentiveness also shows the opposite: it indicates the gaps where value, agency and purpose keep pressing; these too have had to find some place in his scenario after all, however tentatively. That is the nature of reality Hardy felt bound to display to us in his work, whatever his own fluctuating belief or disbelief. That is why, as Tomalin put it, it was indeed a world in which 'he could no longer believe [but] still cherished the memory of belief'.[40]

Julian Barnes' impossible world

But what now happens if we explore the even more disenchanted world of later modernity? How does honest scrutiny view an even more radically godless and purposeless world – the world of Julian Barnes?

This is an even sterner test, for here we move into a different register. Prior to the twentieth century, 'faithless' novelists like Hardy or George Eliot were at least still surrounded with belief. Religion was still a constant reference point for them, still culturally embedded to a significant degree, in spite of progressive disenchantment. It was a context in which religion was still a 'memory of belief', 'something being lost', even though they no longer subscribed to it. In that sense it was still a presence. Whereas for Barnes, although still a general cultural memory, this is now only external. Rather than something lost, it is something never really ever known in the first place – not by immediate personal experience. As one commentator says, 'unlike his 19th century forbears Barnes [as others around him] had no religious faith to lose'.[41] This may be too stark. But it still marks a genuine shift.

Another difference is the declining level of epistemological confidence available. However stark the decline of religious belief (and traditional social order) portrayed in the nineteenth-century novel, there was still a measure of confidence that new knowledge and certainties would supervene. Religious narrative and the authority of old social hierarchies may have been questioned,

---

[40] Tomalin, *The Time-Torn Man*, p. 78.
[41] Andrew Tate, 'An Ordinary Piece of Magic', in Sebastian Groes and Peter Childs (eds), *Julian Barnes* (New York: Continuum, 2011), p. 52.

but it was still assumed that the 'new' thinking would ensure some moral order and moral purpose to replace it. This was particularly true of George Eliot. Even Hardy with his general pessimism, optative mood and incipient ironies, had 'pride in his new thinking' as well as 'the draining away of the old joyous [religious] certitudes'.[42] This was all part of the wider confidence that the realist novelists had gained through the Enlightenment. Their omniscient vantage point released them not just to reject narratives of the past based on religion, myth or social authority, but to adopt new stories. That is why the modern novel was no longer bound to epic handed-down stories from the past, such as classical myths and legends, populated by types of kings, queens, warriors and heroes; instead it could experiment with new stories about 'real' characters based on reason and observation or 'ordinary' credible people from the world around them.[43]

Barnes, however, does not seem so confident about recreating anything. He displays a much more radical unknowing and unease than Hardy's ironies. He not only describes a sensibility in which the props of past certainties – about history, time, identity, God, purpose – have been removed, but also a world in which there seems no expectation of replacing them. For Barnes, no (meta-) narrative at all, whether old or new, is explanatory.[44] Instead, all knowledge is slippery. There is nothing but 'great unrest'.[45] In short, we have moved from a world in which it is difficult to grasp truth, meaning and purpose, to a world where it is virtually impossible. This isn't necessarily a retreat to wholesale constructivism and anti-realism as if there really are no truths of history and personal life to be found at all. The shadow of them sometimes seems to be acknowledged, even if they cannot be grasped.[46] But the shift is still real: there certainly are no *easy* truths discoverable, whether past or future. Not only is the

---

[42] Tomalin, *The Time-Torn Man*, p. 78.

[43] Eric Auerbach attributes this to biblical influence, not just to the aspirations of the Enlightenment: that is, he credits the New Testament story of God incarnate in and amongst ordinary people (as distinct from the warrior King Messiah of myth). The New Testament in that sense is quite different from Homeric epics. See Eric Auerbach, *Mimesis: the Representation of Reality in Western Literature* (Princeton: Princeton University Press, 1953/2003).

[44] In that sense Barnes is expressing 'classic' definitions of postmodernism: cf. J.-L. Lyotard's celebrated description as 'incredulity towards metanarratives'.

[45] The final words in Barnes, *The Sense of an Ending*.

[46] Cf. Lidija Haas, 'Coming of Age', *Times Literary Supplement*, 5 August 2011. Writing about Barnes' *The Sense of an Ending* she claims 'Barnes ... interest in the slipperiness of history and memory is *not* of the postmodern kind. ... There is truth to be found – it's just not always easy to recover' (emphasis mine).

world itself a random and uncertain place – our knowledge and understanding of it is also radically uncertain.

Truth, time, history and narrative: A radical uncertainty

The full texture of this world, as Barnes portrays it, is explored through a number of closely interrelated themes. The diffuse relationship between fact and fiction, the irretrievability of the past, and the problematic nature of time and history are all scrutinized. They are recurring preoccupations of all the novels, part of their warp and weft. They underlie all the narratives of personal relationships and personal identity – which themselves weave, precariously, throughout all the texts. They are conveyed through form as well as content, in experimental structural devices as well as substantive discussion.

For example, in one of Barnes' earlier and most noted works (*Flaubert's Parrot*) the form is so experimental some might say it is not a novel at all.[47] It is part novel, part biography of Flaubert, and part literary criticism: a collage of literary genres. In so far as there is an overall plot it is the effort of a doctor to research the nineteenth-century French writer Flaubert. He is diverted by discovering displays in two museums of a stuffed parrot which was supposed to have sat on Flaubert's desk while he wrote a story. His quest to find the authentic original then leads him to 50 more candidates. But other chapters then interpolate other interests or events without any clear temporal or causal connection. Only the subject Flaubert (or Dr. Braithwaite), themselves uncertain, offer any kind of link at all. This is a structural expression of the blurring of fact and fiction, the inaccessibility and unreliability of the past, the impossibility of reconstructing it – and more generally, the difficulty (or impossibility) of establishing all truth and meaning. We cannot know either 'what really happened' or the significance of what happens.

The choice of Flaubert and Braithwaite as subjects reinforces this. Flaubert was a typical nineteenth-century realist. He was largely in charge of his material and ordered it to tell a story in which things added up and made sense. He wanted and expected to find exact words to express exactly what he wanted. But with Braithwaite Barnes now has a narrator who is almost entirely different. He presents much more uncertainty, worrying that words do not have precise

---

[47] Julian Barnes, *Flaubert's Parrot* (London: Vintage, 1984/2009).

meanings but an uncertain range – and events may turn out differently. This is a deliberate contrast. It shows how far we have travelled since Flaubert, how radically we have to deny past certainties. Does it also imply that there is no meaning, no purposeful 'truth' to be found at all – just randomness? It could do. It certainly pushes us in this direction.

In *A History of the World in 10 ½ Chapters* there is further experiment with structure.[48] Here there are ostensibly 10 short, separate, stories. Some are connected loosely by a common theme (such as a sea voyage), but again there is no chronological sequence of obvious causal connection. In other words we have different tellings of stories with some common themes, but no other obvious way of connecting them purposefully. A discursive essay on the nature of love is then interpolated between chapters 8 and 9 – which by its placing further subverts any temporal or causal connections. In this way even the thematic connections which exist become problematic. Although they may seem significant the structure is pushing us to see they must be random, their 'order' imposed only by our perception rather than objectively there. It reinforces again this perception that this world Barnes inhabits itself resists order. Meaning and purpose is not easily found objectively in the nature of things – and the likelihood is that there is none there to be found. What is hinted at structurally is then also frequently summed up in direct allusion. In the chapter about a nineteenth-century expedition to discover Noah's Ark on Mount Ararat, for example, 'where Amanda discovered in the world divine intent, benevolent order and rigorous justice, her father had seen only chaos, hazard and malice'.[49]

This suspicion, that we create stories and project meaning where none exists, is a familiar one. We already heard it from Richard Dawkins in his railing against the inventions of superstition. Barnes is presenting such a view more in sorrow than anger. For him the projection is an almost inevitable consequence of our uncertainty about 'what is there' and how we might know it, rather than of outright superstition or irrationality. He is also generally much less confident of the distinction between truth and fiction anyway, as we have seen. Nonetheless, it is still clear enough that we are inventing: 'we make up a story to cover the fact we don't know or can't accept'.[50] This is why he offers

[48] Julian Barnes, *A History of the World in 10 ½ Chapters* (London: Vintage, 1989/2009).
[49] Barnes, *History of the World*, p. 148.
[50] Ibid., p. 242.

a 'History' in 'Chapters': that is, deliberately choosing to display history as a partly fictional literary genre, rather than a positive science.[51] It is also why he deliberately offers a semiology (i.e. a system of signs to convey meaning) which blurs the boundaries of textual and visual material: this is precisely to enable us to *make* and *choose* meaning. Thus the chapter in *A History* which recounts the wreck of the ship Medusa tells a 'history' in words with reference to the sign of a picture as well (Géricault's painting *The Raft of the Medusa*). The painting, by its extrapolation from the wider narrative of textual history, sets us free to offer different interpretations which the text would not permit. It frees us to choose and make meaning: if we look at the survivors on the raft: 'do we vote for the optimistic yellowing sky [i.e. ultimate rescue] or for the grieving greybeard [i.e. ultimate tragedy]?'[52] It appears that the choice is ours. This propensity to create meaning does not of itself disprove all objective meaning and purpose. But it certainly creates suspicion that any we claim to find is likely to be illusory.

History, in so far as it is knowable all, is the chief case in point, and in this respect *A History of the World in 10½ Chapters* is especially bleak. The episodes are largely tragic, and the book as a whole, in so far as it has any defining principle to make it a whole, seems based on entropy more than anything else. One summary statement couldn't be more stark: 'Our current model for the universe is entropy, which at the daily level translates as things fuck up.'[53] Thus one commentator: *A History* 'deconstructs the rational, consistent and coherent model for the course of history and replaces it with a sense of entropy which reflects the mutability, discontinuity, arbitrariness and chaos of history'.[54] In short, when Barnes replaces Hardy, when entropy takes the place of evolution and radical epistemological uncertainty replaces confidence in scientific method, the outcome for any purpose in history seems bleaker than ever.

It is much the same for personal history. In *The Sense of an Ending*, a widower approaching old age wants to find some sense of his own history, but cannot. The structure here is less experimental, reverting to a more conventional novel or novella. But the content of the narrative remains similarly ambivalent. Memory and knowledge of personal history, and our responsibilities for it, is as uncertain as public history. The bridge which

---

[51] Cf. Vanessa Guignery, *The Fiction of Julian Barnes* (Basingstoke: Palgrave Macmillan, 2006), p. 67.
[52] Barnes, *History of the World*. Cf. Guignery's discussion, *The Fiction of Julian Barnes*, p. 65.
[53] Barnes, *History of the World*, p. 148.
[54] Guignery, *The Fiction of Julian Barnes*, p. 71.

connects past and present is intrinsically unstable (characters meet on the 'wobbly' Millennium Bridge in London which connects a modern art gallery and a historic cathedral). New 'evidence' about past acts appears in the plot to awaken memories and call into question both the facts of our life and our responsibility for them – but because the narrator himself is unreliable we are still left in doubt what to believe. We are always inventing meaning, for better or worse, and that is the problem: 'when we were young we invented different futures for ourselves; when we are old we invent different pasts for others'.[55] Nor, in any case, can we do anything to resolve what happened, or change ourselves. The main character is teased by the possibility of rerunning time backwards to unravel it all and help heal his remorse (the recurring image here is the water of a tidal bore running upstream against the normal flow). But it cannot happen, because in the end the world is not ordered to help make sense of anything. Like the characters in Hardy's *The Mayor of Casterbridge*, he has to realize this. Neither the reward of merit nor the healing of remorse, is 'life's business'.[56] Beyond the accumulation of experience and (uncertain) personal responsibility there is no meaning that he can discern: only this 'unrest … great unrest'.[57]

The most obvious reason for this is that the metaphysics which might support any more meaning are simply not available. There is no God and no afterlife, either to provide the objective meaning or to provide the possibility of changing it by atonement. In an earlier novel about flying (*Staring at the Sun*) this appears to have been made clear enough. There we find explicit discussion on the possibility and nature of God's existence and what this might offer for reconfiguring our own existence with meaning – but in the end the only 'god' is an indecisive 'general purpose computer' (nicely prefiguring Google!). Nothing beyond that merely human god exists. Not even a great cathedral or the Grand Canyon needs a transcendent God to account for it. The image of flight, which holds this novel together, seems to promise more than these earthbound constraints – but it cannot ultimately deliver. Characters try to fly, but in the end they all 'lose height'.[58]

---

[55] Barnes, *The Sense of an Ending*, p. 80.

[56] Ibid., pp. 59, 82. On *The Mayor of Casterbridge*, see p. 50 above. In the end even Elizabeth, the believer in divine or cosmic justice, had to see that 'there were others receiving less [than her] who had deserved more', Hardy, *The Mayor of Casterbridge*.

[57] Barnes, *The Sense of an Ending*, p. 150.

[58] Julian Barnes, *Staring at the Sun* (London: Vintage, 1986/2009). Flight as a metaphor for transcendence is also used by Barnes in his more directly autobiographical book on ballooning and

The intellectual and emotional honesty in these accounts is often searing. Barnes's widower in *The Sense of an Ending* could have painted his life as the old man in Eliot's *Gerontion*. That is, he could have taken refuge in a sentimental makeover – a fantasy in which he presents himself in more heroic or even just contented terms, fulfilling some serious purpose or calling. That is always the temptation when objective meaning is so elusive – and he was tempted: 'How often do we tell our own life story? How often do we just embellish, make sly cuts? And the longer life goes on, the fewer are those around to challenge our account.'[59] Or else he could at least have pleaded diminished responsibility for his failings: 'I had been its author then, but was not its author now' – and almost does so, because there is *some* justice in that.[60] But he cannot. He cannot entirely deceive himself. He knows this might be 'simply further self-deception.'

There is the same kind of unsparing exactitude when he records his own feelings autobiographically when his wife died, quoting her own words: 'it hurts exactly as much as it is worth … if it didn't matter, it wouldn't matter.'[61] In relation to his (absent) sense of objective purpose, the hurting is the same. It matters to him that he cannot find meaning – but since he honestly cannot find it he will not allow himself any knowing self-deception to relieve that pain.

In all these ways Barnes displays a world as even more inaccessible, and perhaps even more radically purposeless, than Hardy's. He has approached it with the same clear-eyed honesty but in the end has had to convey an even emptier scenario. We may try to do our best within such a godless and purposelessness world – but we can find no answering intention or order from the universe itself. Or so it seems.

Presence in absence: A subversive uncertainty?

But again – is that really all? In fact, like Hardy, there are again some cracks in the picture, and these are inevitable precisely because of the level of irony that Barnes is compelled to employ to respond to the world that he finds. As we

bereavement: cf. *Levels of Life* (London: Jonathan Cape, 2013). There too it takes us nowhere in the end: there is 'No God, no afterlife, no us…', *Levels of Life*, p. 86.
[59] Barnes, *The Sense of an Ending*, p. 95.
[60] Ibid., p. 97
[61] Barnes, *Levels of Life*, p. 71.

have seen, such irony allows everything to be questioned. That in turn must include what appears to be denied or absent. So there is always the possibility of something else. Although this bare possibility of an alternative is hardly a settled answer to what is really there, at least it offers a possible presence, a dialectic with presence rather than just an unremitting absence.[62]

This is exactly what we find. So, for example, at the end of his first novel *Metroland*, where Barnes has largely failed to find meaning and progress for his main character's life, he still doesn't quite give up. He (character and narrator combined) muses on the lights outside the surburban dead end to which he has returned: 'I follow a half-factitious line about the nature of the [street] light; how the sodium with its strength and nearness blots out the effect of even the fullest moon; but how the moon goes on nevertheless; and how this is symbolic of ... well, of something. ...'[63]

He quickly reverts to scepticism: 'but I don't pursue this too seriously: there's no point in trying to thrust false significance on to things.'[64] Even so, he cannot quite let the thought go. The street lamp goes off, but he is still left with a 'lozenge-shaped blue-green after image'.[65] To be sure, that too finally ends, so the (almost) overwhelming verdict remains: there is nothing more, nothing ultimate, nothing beyond our own temporary self-created meanings in life. Yet that after-image has at least been mentioned. It is the ghost of a presence in the absence. So might it return again? It is all part of this 'restlessness' he is still describing even in his latest novel (to date, *The Sense of an Ending*). Nothing is really resolved, not even the conclusion that there is nothing.

This faint presence of some possibility of transcendent meaning haunts all of his novels in some form, even if it is raised mostly to be dismissed. But perhaps it is clearest in that image of flight which dominates *Staring at the Sun*. It is a recurring metaphor for the longing for transcendence. In Barnes's post-Christian world this is not longing for God in any traditional theistic sense. So it is not as specific as Hardy's longing for a cherished memory of a lost belief. But it may be an acknowledgement of precisely that displaced sense of transcendence which Taylor describes (i.e. in the absence of any traditional

---

[62] Cf. Barnes, *Flaubert's Parrot*, p. 89: 'When a contemporary narrator hesitates, claims uncertainty ... does the reader in fact conclude that reality is being more authentically rendered?' It is only a 'technical device', a 'ploy'.

[63] Julian Barnes, *Metroland* (London: Jonathan Cape, 1980), p. 176.

[64] Ibid.

[65] Ibid.

view of God the sense of 'something beyond' has not disappeared entirely but is displaced elsewhere). Here it is transposed into flight from an earthbound existence and its limitations. Taking to an aircraft and flying into the sun expresses through metaphor the sense that even the product of rationality and technology can evoke transcendence.

The text also has other, albeit more bizarre, expressions of the longing. For example, there is the airman's liminal quasi-religious vision of a motor-cyclist riding on the sea below, not dragged down but riding the crest of waves (an allusion to Jesus walking on water). Another example of displaced longing for transcendence is offered in a recollection from childhood. The enigmatic mother Jean remembers being encouraged as a young girl to scream wildly, falling to the ground in a kind of ecstasy, 'half-way to heaven'.[66] It is a defining and cathartic moment, described by one commentator exactly as an act of 'displaced spirituality', a 'kind of wordless prayer'.[67] Later she dismisses it, as she dismisses her son Gregory's turn to faith and mysticism. It is all just a 'roaring at the empty heavens, knowing that however much noise you made, nobody up there would hear you'.[68] Even so, the sound of the scream has been heard. The ecstasy has been recorded. Gregory's non rational, Kiekegaardian faith has at least been noted.

Admittedly the novel keeps bringing us back to earth, structurally and in substantive argument. Aircraft have to land (or crash). When the older Jean is asked by Gregory whether she thinks there is a God she clearly says no: 'we live by just enough light to see that nobody else is there'. For her 'the sky is the limit'. Moreover, Gregory's religious quest carries no obvious conviction. He is a mouthpiece for some sort of faith, but only as a rather two-dimensional figure, a muted voice.

Yet do we not also have to hear the irony here too, at every level? 'The sky is the limit' is itself a *double entendre*. For when mother and son finally take to the sky together at the end of the novel they fly together ambiguously – they are still chasing something. And when the sun keeps glowing over the horizon after it has sunk, this did not signal a final end to the quest. Instead, 'Jean did at last smile towards this post-mortal phosphorescence'.[69] In such ways the novel

---

[66] Barnes, *Staring at the Sun*, pp. 9, 10.
[67] Tate, 'An Ordinary Piece of Magic', p. 53.
[68] Barnes, *Staring at the Sun*, p. 157.
[69] Ibid., p. 195.

'flashes between … enchantment and disenchantment'. Its characters belongs 'to *both* magical and utilitarian worlds'.[70] Barnes, it seems, remains restless.

Another hint of transcendence lies in the very nature of Barnes' storytelling. For all that he refuses the conventional omniscient stance of a realist narrator, its questing nature still resists the more radical postmodern refusal of any possibility of truth. Even though he is acutely aware that meaning keeps slipping and sliding away, whatever techniques one adopts, he still pursues it as if it is 'there'. Thus, for example, although Flaubert's 'true' parrot remains undiscovered, and Flaubert's real voice is indeterminate, the attempt to find them is still important. Likewise in *A History of the World*, where there is certainly no clear, overarching, purpose or meaning available, no definitive history, the title still teases. He is still attempting *History*; that is, stories still keep being told; and as Kathy says in one of them ('The Sunrise'), 'there must be someone to tell the story'. Who? Some god-like narrator(s), if not God, are present again, even in their absence.

Moreover, is there even some hint of an overarching order after all? For all the subversion of order represented by the structure of 10½ very separate chapters, there are also those repeated motifs, like sea voyages, which give it some sort of unity – just as there are repeated phrases and images and ideas which bind together *Flaubert's Parrot* 'like thin bits of gossamer'.[71] In *A History of the World* the ironic mimicry of the Noah's Ark story even insinuates the possibility of a Christian principle of (moral) order, which reappears allusively in some of its other stories as well. At first this seems as though it is going to be only a Darwinian principle of a moral order. Rather like Hardy, it appears that Barnes is telling a story of the world simply according to a Darwinian theory of natural selection and survival of the fittest. But in fact this is subverted. The narrator, the survivor, turns out to be a woodworm. In other words, the lowly survive as the mighty are cast down. So is some moral order being presented here after all, even though ostensibly this history is being told to show there's no obvious order in the history of the world?

---

[70] Carlos Fuentes, 'The Enchanting of the Blue Yonder', Review in *New York Times*, 12 April 1987. Cited in Frederick Holmes, *Julian Barnes* (London: Palgrave Macmillan, 2009), p. 148 (emphasis mine).

[71] Barnes' own phrase in interview with Patrick McGrath, 'Julian Barnes', *Bomb* 21 (1987), quoted in Guignery, *The Fiction of Julian Barnes*, p. 51. Recurring images and themes in *Flaubert's Parrot* include, for example, the idea of coincidence, or whether there is any progress in life, or the way animals offer images for other things.

Of course, irony undercuts this too as an easy option. A woodworm is an unreliable parasite, feeding off religious or scientific paradigms but also subverting them. Overall, then, it remains the case that reality appears generally to have no order. There is no specific way we can read either progress or providence (or circularity) from the 10½ chapters.[72] Even so, these hints of connections and order persist. These 'rhymes' of history and shadowy 'real' narrators remain tantalizing. The specific reward of merit may not be 'life's business' – but there remains this ineradicable sense that life might still have *some* sort of a business.

The meaning and mattering of love

What then is this business of life, if it really exists after all? If, against all odds, there is a purpose perceived, can we name it? There is perhaps just one point above all in his novels where Barnes' own authorial voice appears to address this directly. It is the discourse on love called *Parenthesis* which interrupts *A History of the World*. It is a point at which direct speech cuts through irony. Literary critics might (and do) say it is an intrusion – its form as an essay destroys whatever literary integrity it might otherwise have had as a novel, or set of short stories.[73] But we still have to pay attention. Its direct and peremptory nature demands it. And in any case, the basic theme of love it addresses takes other forms as well, for it is a major preoccupation in his other novels too.[74] Most of all it compels us to take note because it is presented, as nearly as we ever get, as a clear truth claim. At one point love and truth are explicitly compared: 'love and truth, yes, that's the prime connection'.[75]

This might seem to invite just another ironic interpretation. Yet in fact this is precisely where the direct voice of this essay appears to subvert the irony of those previous polyphonic voices. The possibility of truth, previously

---

[72] See especially Claudia Kotte, 'Random Patterns? Orderly Disorder in Julian Barnes's. The Moral Negotiation of Truth in Julian Barnes's *A History of the World in 10 ½ Chapters*', *Arbeiten aus Anglistik und Amerikanistik*, 22.1 (1997), pp. 107–28. I owe this reference to Guignery, *The Fiction of Julian Barnes*.

[73] For general critical reception see summary in Holmes, *Julian Barnes*, pp. 148–9; also Salman Rushdie who specifically regrets that Barnes only talks about love as an essayist here, rather than displaying 'the thing itself' as a novelist: Salman Rushdie, *Imaginary Homelands: Essays and Criticism, 1981–1991* (London: Granta Books, 1991), pp. 242–3.

[74] Notably, *Before She Met Me* (1982), *Talking It Over* (1991) and *Love etc* (2000): it is also significant in *The Sense of an Ending*.

[75] Barnes, *A History of the World*, p. 245.

deconstructed, now appears curiously reinstated: 'We all know objective truth is not obtainable. … But while we know this, we must still believe that objective truth is obtainable; or we must believe that it is 99 per cent obtainable; or if we can't believe this we must believe that 43 per cent objective truth is better than 41 per cent'.[76]

In short, when love is being compared to truth it is 'real' truth that he has in mind: objective truth. Moreover, Barnes, wanting as ever to be precise, is willing to press his case by defining further. He is clear that this love is *not* just a necessary function of evolutionary survival. Nor is it 'something which makes you happy' (it doesn't, in any case!). Nor is it just reducible to pheromones.[77] It is, precisely, itself – distinctively and really itself, and in that sense it is a real truth. As such Barnes appears to accept here the ultimate authority of love with rare univocity. For all its disappointments and failings it retains distinctiveness and it matters uniquely. It even has a transcendent quality. It outranks both religion and art. Religion has become 'either wimpishly workaday or terminally crazy'. Art 'announces its transcendence of the world … but isn't accessible to all'. Love, by contrast, 'gives us our humanity, and also our mysticism. …' It shows us that '*there is more to us than us*'.[78]

The concluding reflections of the essay reinforce the point. They tell us that love is something we 'must' believe in as we believe in nothing else. Barnes's default setting of equivocation still intrudes, but the dramatic force still remains at the end with the positive meaning of love. It is embodied in the evocative image of two intertwined sleepers. Thus:

> And so it is with love. We must believe in it, or we're lost. We may not obtain it, or we may obtain it and find it renders us unhappy; we must still believe in it. If we don't, then we merely surrender to the history of the world and to someone' else's truth. It will go wrong, this love; it probably will. … Our current model for the universe is entropy. … But when love fails us, we must still go on believing in it. … Yes, that's right, it can be done, we can face history down. Excited, I stir and kick. She shifts and gives a subterranean, a subaqueous sigh. Don't wake her. It seems a grand truth now, though in the

---

[76] Ibid., pp. 245–6. Cf. Gregory Salyer: Barnes offers 'the paradox of subverting objective truth and then reinstalling it'. 'One Good story leads to another: Julian Barnes's *A History of the World in 10 ½ Chapters*', *Literature and Theology*, 5.2 (1991), p. 228: quoted by Guignery, *The Fiction of Julian Barnes*, p. 68.

[77] Barnes, *A History of the World*, p. 245.

[78] Ibid., pp. 244–5 (emphasis mine).

morning it may not seem worth disturbing her for. She gives a gentler, lesser sigh. I sense the map of her body beside me in the dark. I turn on my side, make a parallel zigzag, and wait for sleep.[79]

It is a telling intervention into this particular novel. This half chapter reinstates what so much (though not quite all) of the other ten chapters either deny or dispute. It displays the presence of an apparently irresistible meaning.

To be sure, this still does not have to be taken as a transcendent meaning implying a wider metaphysics of purpose. This love relates to particular finite persons, so the purpose it generates might itself seem only finite and relative. It is not necessarily related to, or dependent on, any transcendent or overarching purpose. In his autobiographical account of bereavement this becomes explicit: the longing of a lost love is not *sehhnsucht* (i.e. a longing for something undefinable); it is exactly the longing for some particular person.[80] Even so, the language and images used are surely still straining to express more. For we 'must' go on believing in it, we are told. And that 'must' hints at an almost metaphysical necessity after all. It calls to mind again Critchley's analysis of moral experience. The force of love we feel, like the force of moral imperative, may derive from our experience of particular persons – but it conveys an absoluteness which goes beyond their finite empirical reality.[81]

Such a sense that love can and must 'face down' failure, time, history, even death, resonates widely. To return briefly to Hardy, it certainly finds echoes there. For with Hardy too, love represented a purpose with almost god-like powers. It had power to create human identity, and a meaning which even transcends its own end. It received fairly straightforward expression in the more benign world of his early work, *Far From the Madding Crowd*, in the power of Gabriel Oak's love for Bathsheeba. But it is equally true in the darker plots of *The Mayor of Casterbridge*. There even Henchard lives for a love, not just power and status. Although flawed and frustrated, both by Henchard's own character and circumstance, it has still given him his depth and even grandeur as a character. This transcendent significance of love is even more explicit in *Jude*. Sue's sacrificial parting from Jude prompts an exchange about the deepest of all loves, the *agape* of St Paul's eulogy to love

---

[79] Ibid. p. 246.
[80] Barnes, *Levels of Life*, p. 112.
[81] See p. 33 above.

in 1 Corinthians 13, which is the only thing that 'endures for ever.' For 'in that chapter' says Jude, ' we are at one, ever-beloved darling, and on it we'll part friends. Its verses will stand fast when all the rest that you call religion has passed away!'.[82]

There are other resonances too. Thornton Wilder's haunting story *The Bridge of San Luis Rey*, almost contemporary with Hardy, is particularly notable. For this too investigates providence and the meaning of events, and largely fails to find it – but does find love. Set in eighteenth- century Peru, a freak accident prompts a priest to examine the lives of the five victims in order to demonstrate the divine meaning of the event for each – and like the characters of Hardy and Barnes he has to admit defeat. But something is still found. What emerges, for each of those lives, is a narrative of mattering, of loving and being loved, however falteringly or fleetingly. That narrative then becomes the generator of meaning, even for the accident. So the book ends with this celebrated, meditation on the transcendent nature of love:

> Soon ... all memory of those five will have left the earth, and we ourselves shall be loved for a while and forgotten. But the love will have been enough; all those impulses of love return to the love that made them. ... There is a land of the living and the land of the dead, and the bridge is love, the only survival, the only meaning.[83]

Wider implications

Such is the presence of objective purpose and meaning which Hardy and Barnes display. It is only a ghost of a meaning. Overall it remains the case that their worlds are without such purpose, and without God. Yet they still include these half-hints of idealism and transcendent purpose, especially in the depth and infinite demands of human relationship, and in love. So in the end no amount of equivocation can entirely deflect this. A vestige of objective and transcendent purposiveness does remain – part of the scenario which scientism or materialism cannot adequately account for.[84]

---

[82] Hardy, *Jude*, p. 438.
[83] Thornton Wilder, *The Bridge of San Luis Rey* (London: Penguin Classics, 2000), p. 124.
[84] For Barnes the implications of these moral and human experiences specifically for subverting the reductionism of science are not so significant, for he has already moved on from Hardy's struggle

I do not wish to claim too much from these observations. They are not experiences of purpose which strictly require a metaphysical home. They certainly haven't moved us to Clark's more confident assertion that 'we *have* to include in our scenario the thought that God is working His purpose out'. In that strict sense, as Clark himself is well aware, the vision that there is some kind of objective intended meaning in everything (an 'all-unity of the cosmos', as he calls it) is *not* part of everyone's present experience, let alone that of Hardy and Barnes. It is more like a 'task and a promise', not an 'uncomplicated fact'.[85]

Nonetheless, this literary detour has shown us more how the texture of our sense of purpose presses its case. Even in godless scenarios it shows how it makes its presence felt. Even in silence it demonstrates its strange eloquence. It shows not only loss but some sort of recovery; a sense of narrative and moral purpose which persists even when a facile sense of order, purpose and providence has disappeared. As with our survey of intellectual history, it helps display its enduring authority, and even its sense of transcendence. And as such it must now bring us to the theological task itself. It naturally leads to an exploration of how this sense of transcendent purpose appears specifically and explicitly in the theological tradition as *God's* purpose.

with this; he is not so mesmerized by the challenge of scientism. Nonetheless, its logic still remains relevant in this respect, as in others.

[85] Clark, *God's World and The Great Awakening*, pp. 186–7.

3

Purpose and Providence in Theology: Roots and Developments of a Core Belief

This turn to theology is not to introduce a new subject or to set the scene in an entirely new way. Theology already belongs to the sense of purpose which we have tracked in intellectual history and literary expression. The common thread is hardly surprising. I have already noted how a wider history of ideas interacts with different conceptions of God when belief in God is explicit. Neoplatonism, realism, voluntarism, natural science and postmodernism, have all been a matrix for this. I also noted how implicit signs of God have operated in that wider history. The main drivers of purpose – our sense of necessity, narrative, moral mattering, transcendence – are all potentially theological in character, even when functioning in secular social and literary contexts. In that sense theology has already been part of the discussion about purpose, its turns to history and self, and its deconstructions.

But a more focused turn to theology is still necessary. It is important, first, simply as a reminder of a tradition. We need to acknowledge just how rooted and central the notions of purpose and God's personal agency have been in Christian theism – especially through the doctrine of providence. This tradition has had high profile in the past in the classic canons of Western theology, but has suffered a certain 'aura of neglect' more recently.[1] So it deserves more attention. It is also important because theology will re-frame some of the issues. A sense of objective purpose which persists *theologically* does so for distinctive reasons and in distinctive ways – as well as overlapping with those wider stories.

[1] Murphy and Ziegler (eds), *The Providence of God*, p. 1. Perhaps this relative neglect is because it has never been a credal doctrine. Yet in fact it can claim to underlie all the other actual doctrines of the creed. Cf. Brian Hebblethwaite, *Philosophical Theology and Christian Doctrine* (Oxford: Blackwell, 2005), p. 132. There are some recent signs of its rehabilitation however: cf. Mark Elliott, *Providence Perceived* (New York: De Gruyter, 2015); this was published too late to take full account of it here.

What follows now is a review of this theological terrain. It reminds us of some of the basic roots and developments of the classic tradition of providence in the Western canon. I am well aware that this canon is by no means the whole of theology, so it is a waymark not necessarily the final destination. But it remains important to take soundings there. It is where God's purposive agency, as the basis for all purpose, has been most extensively scrutinized. It is a place where key issues emerge and can be considered more systematically. As such it is a necessary basis, even if not sufficient, for all re-imaginings of providence which will also be needed.

Foundations in scriptural narrative

The heart of this tradition lies, naturally, in biblical foundations.[2] The largely narrative form of the scriptures witnesses immediately to the idea of a personal and purposive God. In both Hebrew Bible and New Testament, experience of the divine is conveyed pre-eminently in narrative form as an experience of a personal reality who is a purposive agent.[3]

This does not make it anthropomorphic or crudely reductionist. 'God' in scripture is still *sui generis*. God's being is almost always presented opaquely and obliquely, a unique and hidden 'I am' presented without spatial or temporal detail, in spite of the setting in concrete human history and embodiment (as such this God is quite distinct from the obviously anthropomorphized fictional gods of other religious stories, as Auerbach has famously argued[4]). Even so, this mysterious and transcendent divine reality is still represented as one who 'speaks' and 'acts' in personal ways. God is not just an ultimate origin of things but a purposive mover of things and people by personal relationship with them. 'God' is the one who brings people out of one place and time into another; from the garden to the desert to Gethsemane to resurrection; from exile to homeland; and finally from this age to a new heaven and earth.

---

[2] The term 'providence' is not itself particularly scriptural; but the notions of divine purpose, foresight, provision, and rule, to which it refers, are shot through both Hebrew Bible and New Testament.

[3] The intrinsic, analytic, relationship between 'person' and 'purposive agency' is well stated in recent philosophical theology by R. H. King in *The Meaning of God* (London: SCM Press, 1974). The form of narrative to convey this has been widely and variously explored, and here Hans Frei is especially helpful. See further discussion of this later in this chapter, pp. 102–3 (especially note 81); also pp. 126–8.

[4] Auerbach, *Mimesis*.

This agency is uniquely effective and widespread. It extends as a purposive rule over all creation, nature, history and individual lives, inescapable and pervasive. As such it is, again, no simple extension of finite agency: it is *sui generis*. Yet it still remains characteristically personal in form; that is to say, this effective fulfilment of God's purpose is carried out primarily by personal interaction with creatures and their purposes, not simply by impersonal fiat. It is within this complex and 'covenantal' relationship that the meaning of providence emerges: that is, as the articulation of the purposive agency of a personal God which gives meaning and purpose to all finite reality and agency, but without replacing or overwhelming it.

In both the natural world and human world the purpose of this providential activity is a creative and redemptive love. It is also universal. It is worked out in relation to every kind of event and object, both in their generalities and on specific occasions. Thus in the natural world, God provides generally through 'seed-time and harvest', through grain, bread and fishes; but God also summons the winds, parts the sea of reeds, stills the waves, on specific occasions. In human history the pattern is similar. Both nations and individual people are all subject to God's purposes in general and specific ways. Within that interaction human capacity to resist or form separate purposes is real, but this resistance is still consistently used or 'overruled' to fulfil ultimate divine ends. This pattern is implicit throughout the narratives, but also sometimes made explicit. The editor's summary of the story of Joseph and his brothers in the patriarchal narratives is characteristic; it was not the brothers who sent Joseph to exile but God: 'even though you intended to do harm to me, God intended it for good'.[5]

Such patterns of providence are shown in particular sub-narratives, but also in the metanarratives of history. The whole history of the people of Israel is an exemplar. They are called, led, chastened, but never ultimately forsaken, through the *whole* of their long experience of wilderness, exile and return. This meta-pattern includes peoples outside Israel as well. In the view of the eighth-century prophet Amos it was God who brought up the Philistines from Caphtor and the Syrians from Kir, as well as Israel from Egypt.[6] In Isaiah it is

---

[5] Gen. 50.20.
[6] Amos 9.7.

the non-Israelite Cyrus who is anointed as an instrument of God's purposes.[7] In other words there is an effective divine purpose at work which is always universal in scope, at every level, and in every kind of event.

This overall pattern is then decisively endorsed in the New Testament in Jesus Christ, who is both an individual and representative figure. The narrative of Christ confirms the radical particularity of divine action in relation to individuals: in Christ attention is paid to individuals in the crowd and to 'every sparrow which falls'. Equally, it confirms its universal scope: God in Christ 'draws *all* people to himself'. It reinforces its effectiveness too. Even when creaturely resistance seems implacable, God's action in Christ achieves its purposes. So even as Pilate and others oppose Jesus, and appear to defeat God's purposes in him, they still find themselves contributing to God's ultimate ends (of redemption). This power of God's purposes even in apparent defeat is most especially in the Johanine accounts of the passion: 'you would have no power over me unless it had been given to you from above'.[8]

None of this in any way denies the counter narratives of scripture which emphasize the radical nature of evil and resistance to God's purposes. These show there is no straightforward linear doctrine of progress. Instead, there are many stories of continuing rise and fall, with the fulfilment of the kingdom of God belonging as much to the 'next' world as to this. Nor does scripture deny the devastating effect within human experience of these counter stories, and the inevitable apophaticism about the nature of God's purposes in some particular events. It includes the profound laments of Job, the Psalmists, and the sense of abandonment and incomprehension of Jesus himself. Nonetheless, the overall datum of God's purpose remains. Whatever evil, resistance, bewilderments, exist, God's good purpose still ultimately accommodates them all, in some way.

A *locus classicus* for scripture's own theological reflection on this pattern lies in Paul's theology of history in Romans 9–11. Here there is a key worked example of the way, ultimately, '*all* things work together for good'.[9] For even God's rebellious people will eventually be grafted back in to God's overall will. In this way the God who has 'imprisoned all in disobedience' may also be 'merciful to all' (Ch. 11). The inscrutability and mystery of the providential

---

[7] Isa. 45.
[8] Jn 19.11.
[9] Rom. 8.28 (emphasis mine).

working is fully acknowledged – 'how unsearchable are his judgements and how inscrutable his ways'. But this does not dilute confidence in its reality and effectiveness. Its ontological basis is a conception of God 'from whom, through whom, and to whom, are *all* things'.[10] Its epistemological basis is in Christ who demonstrated this being and character of God in history, the one through whom *all* things are both 'created' and 'reconciled'.[11]

Such is the overall conviction about divine purposive rule that scripture conveys. I shall return to it later in the light of subsequent theological reflection – there is more to be said about the specific shapes of divine purpose it displays. For now it is enough to register just how pervasive it is in general terms. This basic notion of an overruling purpose of divine agency, concerned for particulars, interacting rather than imposing, often bewildering yet actually effective on the widest possible scale and scope, is a vital part of scriptural faith.[12] Its *prima facie* force was evident for the pre-critical mind. Even with critical tools to hand it remains just as striking, for it does not belong to any one editorial hand or one strand of biblical history – it is woven in to a whole variety of narrative traditions. For the same reason a post-critical reading cannot ignore it either. As such, 'providence' in some sense is inescapably scriptural. It is certainly not just an invention of later theology.

Justin and Augustine – the personal God's rule of the part, the whole, history and eternity

But how did early Christian theology then begin to unfold this scriptural theme? On the one hand it clearly had to relate to a wider world of thought and experience. Here the most obvious early resource was Stoic philosophy.[13] Stoic belief that natural laws determine everything to some good purpose, as we saw in the first chapter, was already prevalent. So this sense of a 'natural' moral purpose could be easily re-expressed as the purposive rule of a personal God – it provided a ready structure for Christian theology to annex. In particular,

[10] Rom. 9.1–11.31, 36 (emphasis mine).
[11] Col. 1.15, 20.
[12] 'Both Old and New Testaments may be read as a sustained testimony to God's lordship over all things, which is what the biblical notion of providence amounts to': Gorringe, *God's Theatre*, p. 5.
[13] Cf. the account in David Fergusson, 'The Theology of Providence', *Theology Today*, 67 (2010), pp. 261–78.

the sense of necessity in natural law connected easily with the conviction that God's will was sovereign and universal. A purpose being worked out in the world could more readily be imagined for all people (living and dead) if it was now conceived to be in the hands of an omnipotent and personal God.[14]

On the other hand, early theology also had to work out its distinctiveness from surrounding philosophy. In particular, it had to distinguish the personal nature of the divine rule from the impersonal nature of an inexorable fate, especially in its interaction with ourselves as persons. It needed to distinguish the way a personal God makes provision for individuals in their particular circumstances and actions, rather than just imposing some overall state of affairs.

So we find early apologist Justin Martyr emphasizing just this balance. He assumed a connection with wider philosophy but also made these clear points of differentiation. He stressed the non-necessity of divine personal action and its concern for the particular:

> there seem to be seeds of truth among all men; but they are charged with not accurately understanding [the truth] ... what we say about future events being foretold, we do not say it as if they came about by a fatal necessity; but God foreknowing all that shall be done by all men, and it being His decree that the future actions of men shall all be recompensed *according to their several value*.[15]

As we have seen, later philosopher-theologians operating in a Stoic tradition (like Spinoza) did not always take this fully on board: 'God wills the whole not the part'. But Justin was clear enough. The value of the individual is a vital implication of Christian insistence that the purpose we encounter is truly personal. It marks out one of the most distinctive characteristics of an authentic Christian theology of providence from its earliest days: it is personal and particular, as well as universal.

This inclusive scope of providence – embracing the individual and particular within a purpose for all things – became even more notable in Augustine's much more comprehensive treatment.[16] He developed the doctrine in at least three distinct ways.

---

[14] Cf. Theophilus of Antioch, *To Autolycus*, Book 2, 38 (cited in Fergusson, 'The Theology of Providence').

[15] Justin Martyr, *First Apology*, 44 (emphasis mine).

[16] The universal scope of providence in Augustine is threaded throughout his writings. See, for example, Augustine, *City of God*, 5: 11.

First, in the *Confessions*, he writes especially about this personal and particular mode of providence. He sees the narrative of his own life as a series of events specifically steered by God in order to fulfil a wider purpose of God. A celebrated example is his intellectual and spiritual journey from Manicheism to Christian faith, which he sees to be guided by God through a combination of 'internal' and 'external' events. He has an internal desire to leave Carthage and go to Rome. This physical journey is then facilitated by the external phenomenon of favourable winds.[17] For the modern mind this raises all sorts of issues about the nature of causality. God's specific causal involvement with the wind is problematic for us; the notion that God internally 'caused' Augustine's own desires also raises difficult issues of personal responsibility (for Augustine as well as for ourselves). So we shall need to look at causality later. But for now what is notable is simply this early theological emphasis on the personal and particular: divine action is no mere abstraction or generality; it is conceived concretely, personally and in particular events.

Augustine's second development of providence then ranges much more widely. He gave sustained attention to the narratives of history – and in that sense laid pre-modern foundations for the later turn to history.[18] This is clearest in *The City of God* where theological reflection is set against a background of momentous historical events rather than personal narrative.

How was this worked out? To begin with, the conversion of Constantine and the potential role of the empire in furthering the kingdom of God meant that ordinary empirical history was being seen as straightforwardly providential. The outcomes of human history were, after all, looking more and more obviously like a direct outcome of God's purposes, culminating in the visible triumph of the church. Teleology, the fulfilment of divine purpose for humanity, seemed to be working out in human history seamlessly, without disruption. And Augustine first seemed to accept this interpretation.[19] It was easy to assume that God's moral purposes for good were, self-evidently, being achieved by the state in the visible workings of history. This also allowed him to follow a largely sanguine Neoplatonic and Aristotelian view about the value of the state as a 'school' for virtue and human flourishing.

---

[17] Augustine, *Confessions*, 5, 7, 8, 13. Cited in Michael Langford, *Providence* (London: SCM, 1981).
[18] A key element in clearing the ground for a more serious engagement with history was his critique of merely cyclical views of time: see, for example, *City of God*, 12: 13–15.
[19] At this point Augustine was following the early Christian historian Eusebius.

But of course this particular interpretation of history could not last. When the empire came under attack and Rome was sacked, this unruffled view of providence became untenable. The purposes of God could no longer be read off unproblematically from the progress of the earthly state, nor could that state be, straightforwardly, a school for virtue in which a fulfilment could be achieved.

Yet that did not mean history itself receded from Augustine's view; it remained as an arena for God's purposes to be worked out. What it required was a more nuanced account of those purposes, in which a theology of divine sovereignty and purpose could incorporate the darker side of history and all its contrary trajectories. And this is what Augustine provided. He allowed for deferral of meaning, in which it as much harder to read God's purposes from ordinary linear sequences. This did not mean reducing the scope of divine sovereignty per se, but it did mean a change in the way this sovereignty is worked out. It had to be understood in a more indirect way, as a divine purpose working towards ends which are not always empirically evident. In line with those biblical foundations, it had to work through all kinds of events and people, not just those which are owned or motivated by explicit religious faith.[20] God continued to work in history, but that work did not proceed by any facile doctrine of straightforward progress.

These ambiguities of history also meant shifting more emphasis onto a final *telos* beyond history altogether. Again, this did not evacuate historical events as such of meaning, but it did defer the fulfilment of the meaning they carried to a transcendent frame of reference. This too implied a measure of agnosticism; the fact *that* divine purposes were being worked out in particular historical events was not disputed, but *what* they were was no longer so clear. So much so that it history is now quite fairly considered as a problem: 'with Augustine ... the question of the meaning of the sequence of history's events poses itself as a central theological *problem*, both with regard to the events of an individual's own life, and with regard to the events that constitute history as a whole'.[21]

---

[20] Cf., for example, Augustine, *City of God*, 5: 21.
[21] Cf. Langdon Gilkey, *Reaping the Whirlwind: A Christian Interpretation of History* (New York: Seabury Press, 1976), p. 165 (emphasis mine). Cf. also Raymond Plant, *Politics, Theology and History* (Cambridge: Cambridge University Press, 2001), where this is quoted.

Even so, this necessarily inscrutable *telos* beyond history never replaced the necessity of history itself. Religion was still the *historia* of divine providence – rather than merely a screen on which timeless truths can be apprehended.[22] Moreover, divine sovereignty in history also remained explicit and central, although redefined. This was secured precisely by divine transcendence of history and time, as well as activity within it. An effective ordering of all events in time is grounded in God's knowledge of our history from beyond time, in an eternity in which time appears 'all at once'.[23] It is an interesting example of the great tectonic plates of a scriptural belief and a wider philosophy (i.e. Platonism) being brought together – but more in mutual reinforcement than in tension, at least in this instance.

The third development of providence emerged as Augustine cast an even wider, cosmic, net for his thinking. This is a more oblique take on providence but potentially even more radical, setting the divine *telos* in an even broader frame. It is most obvious in *De Doctrina Christiana* where Augustine expounds the whole of temporal reality as a 'sign' (*signum*) of God. At root this derived from the prior conception of God as uniquely undetermined: that is, a reality who alone is sufficient, not pointing beyond himself but existing (and to be enjoyed) in and for himself. The corollary of this is that everything else does exist in relation to and for the sake of something else – namely, this wholly undetermined God.[24] As such everything is indeed 'intended' or 'meant' as a sign of God; the purpose of everything is to exist ultimately 'for God'.

This does not provide a narrative of providence in conventional historicized terms. In principle it could be construed without reference to temporality or historicality. That is, things and events could relate 'vertically' to God as signs, without reference to their own context in history. But in practice Augustine's view of all reality as sign was based on the supremely historical sign of the incarnation – so in fact all signs only work by showing the fulfilment of things in a historically conditioned relation to God. Rowan Williams' illuminating essay on *De Doctrina* summarizes:

> The Word's taking of flesh is not a dissolving of history as eternal truth takes over some portion of the world. ... Rather the incarnation manifests the

---

[22] *City of God* is the main focus for Augustine's use of history but see also *De Vera Religione*, 7.13.
[23] See my further exposition of this sort of view in Chapter 4: pp. 131–2 below.
[24] Augustine, *De Doctrina Christiana*, 22.

essential quality of the world itself as 'sign' or trace of its maker. It instructs us once and for all that we have our identity within the shifting mobile realm of representation, non-finality, growing and learning, because it reveals what the spiritual eye ought to perceive generally – *that the whole creation is uttered and 'meant' by God*, and therefore has no meaning in itself. ... Only when, by the grace of Christ, we know that we live entirely in a world of signs are we set free for the restlessness that is our destiny. ...[25]

This is a postmodern take on Augustine's pre-modern theology, but it encapsulates its texture well. It is the depiction of a world of things and events which do not settle easily in themselves but only in relation to something beyond themselves: that is, to God. This relation cannot be read off straightforwardly from empirical reality, but nor is it to be read off without reference to empirical reality, for only in the historicity of Christ is that relation fully established. What is most striking, however, is the cosmic scope of what the christic rubric for reading reality supports. Christ the *logos* is a sign for *all* personal life, world history, creation – all that is. In Christ all this is specifically 'meant', by God and for God's purposes; so it sets a context in which the purposes of God in providence must reach to, literally, everything.

Such, then, are the key features of early Christian theology as it developed its distinct doctrine of providence. A general sense of necessity is interpreted as the will of a sovereign, personal, free God, rather than fate. The instinct to relate purpose to both the particular and universal is now rooted in the will of a God who is himself both personal and cosmic in scope of action, rather than left without a metaphysical home. The problematics of finding of purpose in history when progress fails are referred to the transcendent frame of these divine purposes; and the hermeneutical issue which then arises (i.e. identifying this divine purpose) is given a distinctive key in the particularity and historicity of the Christ's incarnation, which secures some empirical point of reference rather than retreating totally to apophaticism (yet doesn't diminish its universal scope because this historical Christ is also the eternal Word). This last point would have to await the later more radical turn to history and narrative to be fully developed. But its foundations were certainly laid here.

---

[25] Rowan Williams, 'Language, Reality and Desire in Augustine's *De Doctrina*', *Journal of Literature and Theology*, 3 (1989), p. 141 (emphasis mine).

Medieval concerns: Systematic theology and causality in Thomas Aquinas

Moving now to the developments of the medieval era, many of these foundations were naturally carried forward. But two new issues in particular also deserve attention. Both have proved significant for understanding providence in the longer term – and as we shall see Aquinas proved a key figure for both.

As theology developed systematically, the first issue was to locate providence properly in relation to other doctrines. This mattered because it showed the significance of providence; it demonstrates how the doctrine became so centrally rooted in theology. Here Aquinas helps immediately, for he located providence in two places. He placed it in the doctrine of creation, to enable him to express providence as God's 'government' of creation (carried out through other creatures and supremely through Christ). But he also located it in God himself, specifically the will of God.[26] Locating it there as the *ratio ordinis rerum in finem* (i.e. as the right ordering of all things according to their final end) emphasized its significance even further – precisely because it shows that it originates and ends *in God*.[27]

This double location helped ensure that providence was kept rooted in the ultimacy and perfection of the divine mind and will, even though operative in and through the contingent affairs of this world. This in turn was a way of safeguarding the radical scope and effectiveness of this providence: that is, securing the meaning of providence as the expression of a sovereign will and purpose in any and every state of affairs, however contingent they may seem to us. It could and must include, for example, the ordering of what are (to us) only future contingents: that is, hypothetical states of affairs or narratives in the future. Even this could be part of providence precisely because it was held to lie in God's eternal mind and will. As such, this prevented any reduction of objective divine activity in creation and redemption to the subjective responses of human agency and experience – the sort of criticism which was later to be directed at nineteenth-century liberal theology.[28] It was also an expression of Aquinas's determination to hold together personal categories of God (that is,

---

[26] Thomas Aquinas, *Summa Theologiae*, 1a 22.
[27] Ibid.
[28] Cf. John Webster, 'On the Theology of Providence', in Murphy and Ziegler (eds), *The Providence of God*, pp. 158–78.

a God who acts in the world) with the *sui generis* transcendent nature of God (i.e. a God whose action springs from an ultimacy which belongs only to God). God acts, but not as 'a' person existing as we do.[29]

The second issue which pressed in this period was causality. A revival of interest in Aristotelian philosophy, mediated by Arab philosophers, had brought this to the surface. Here again Aquinas was a key figure. In response to these pressures of Arab influence, he presented a distinctive account of causality, especially as it functioned in providence. This picked up the issue of necessity, endorsing Justin's concern that it must be distinguished from blind fate and determinism, but also re-weaving it to open up new and fertile understandings of causality.

How did Aquinas carry this out? Arab philosophy had appropriated Aristotle in a particular way, tending to all-embracing determinism; like the Stoics, it included both God and the natural order in a single order of necessity.[30] Aquinas, in contrast, acknowledged some of Aristotle's schema but also made important distinctions between different kinds of causation, in order to resist the full determinist logic of some Arabic reinterpretation. The celebrated distinction between primary and secondary causality opened up the possibility of a conceptual and theological space between divine and creaturely action. It permitted some account of creaturely action and responsibility, while retaining a strong doctrine of divine sovereignty.

On the one hand this allowed Aquinas to assert that a personal God can operate through the secondary action of natural and human agents without reducing their causality simply to divine causality. That is to say, neither natural nor human agency is just a necessary outworking of the divine order (the 'One'), but has its own kind of causality – opening up the possibility of studying natural causes in their own terms. On the other hand the notion of primary causality also allowed Aquinas to retain the absolute primacy of God's knowledge and will in all things, including secondary causality: for 'all things act in the power of God himself'.[31] In this way God can act 'interiorly' in *all*

---

[29] How these can be held together, and whether they can be, especially in relation to the doctrine of divine simplicity, is the subject of continuing debate and a vast literature: for a recent defence, see, for example. James Dolezal, *God Without Parts: Divine Simplicity and the Metaphysics of God's Absoluteness* (Eugene, OR: Wipf & Stock, 2011).

[30] The tendency to determinism was not all embracing for all Arabic thought. It is important to recognize that other Islamic thought was wary of it, not least because it implied an abstract form of reasoning.

[31] Aquinas, *Summa Theologiae*, 1a 105.1.

things (i.e. not just occasionally in miracles as 'something that happens outside the whole realm of nature').[32] In short, God can act effectively through the agency of creatures in every sequence of events which unfold in time. Thus: 'Divine providence not only disposes what effects will take place, but also the manner in which they will take place, and which actions will cause them.'[33]

As with Augustine, it is God's metaphysical platform in eternity, in which divine knowledge and will are one, from which this all-embracing scope of action ultimately derives. But it also derives from this analysis of causation, which gives it more conceptual clarity. It was a significant achievement. It provided a view of divine providence where divine sovereignty is uncompromised, while retaining the personal nature of a God who genuinely interacts with other agents. As such it could be distinguished from the impersonal fate of Stoic philosophy, or the all-embracing determinism of some Arab philosophy. So much so it has been hailed as a theological defence against Arab philosophy equivalent to Martel's military defence of Christendom against Arab armies at Poitiers in AD 732.[34] It can also be credited with opening up new possibilities for natural science.

To be sure, this would not satisfy all. The tensions of necessity and freedom would not be resolved so easily. A primary–secondary distinction in causality has to be very robust to incorporate all the issues involved convincingly, but in reality the relative autonomy of secondary causality is conceptually fragile. It easily collapses unless the nature of divine causality is buttressed by a more radical doctrine of divine transcendence which can distinguish primary divine causation as a wholly different kind of causality, that is, one which does not 'compete' at all with creaturely causality. But if this transcendent path is taken, it then implies a kind of divine action which could barely be counted as 'cause' at all. It would be only a very remote analogy of causation, an 'analogy to the point of apophasis' as David Bentley Hart has put it.

That may not ultimately matter. In fact, for Hart, *only* such a radically transcendent sense of divine causality allows for the important distinction between events which are divinely willed and divinely permitted (a necessary

---

[32] Ibid.
[33] Ibid., 2a2ae 80–91.
[34] E. H. Gilson, 'St Thomas Aquinas', *Proceedings of the British Academy*, 21 (1935): cited in Langford, *Providence*. The military metaphor is, perhaps, not entirely appropriate – but it does draw attention to its perceived significance.

distinction if providence is to be properly distinguished from determinism).[35] Yet at the time, in this period immediately before modernity, this metaphysics of 'absolute' transcendence and radically analogical thinking was actually declining (leading some to suggest that causality is a not a helpful category anyway).[36] So in that sense much more needed to be done to support it. It either required more elaboration and defence of radical transcendence, or more analysis of causality itself – or both.

Another unresolved issue was the meaning of sovereignty. As an assumption of classical theism it was not negotiable, at least in general terms. But it required more definition if these kinds of divine causality are to operate meaningfully without collapsing entirely back into determinism – and this did not happen sufficiently. As we shall see, more recent theology has indeed redefined and re-imagined sovereignty – mostly in response to pressures of theodicy but also precisely because of these underlying problems of framing a divine causality which does not overwhelm the creature. However, these later re-writings of sovereignty have been mostly reductionist: that is, reducing its scope and meaning in a way not open to Aquinas, and (arguably) inadequate to any theism. So the issue remains.

This naturally raises the question – might there be other ways to resolve it? For example, rather than diluting the meaning of divine sovereignty, could Hart's expanded and more radical meaning of transcendence deal with this? Might not a truly radical transcendence of time allow effective fulfilment of divine purposes within time by re-framing the context of human action to include this transcendent dimension (rather than by compromising the integrity of our own causality)?[37] Aquinas would not have demurred, but did not frame the issue in exactly this way, and later neo-Thomists positively resisted it. So this too is an issue to which we shall need to return.

---

[35] David Bentley Hart, 'Providence and Causality: On Divine Innocence', in Murphy and Ziegler (eds), *The Providence of God*, pp. 34–6. Arguably, Aquinas himself was alert to this, but neo-Thomists were not.

[36] Cf. Katherine Sonderegger: 'Thomas Aquinas developed a delicate doctrine of "secondary causality", a notion that, in my view, empties and radically reworks the very idea of cause. … A proper doctrine of providence will learn from these reworking of divine causality: but even more it will resist the root notion of cause altogether'. 'The Doctrine of Providence', in Murphy and Ziegler (eds), *The Providence of God*, p. 150.

[37] This sort of option, which Hart has hinted, is expounded in Chapter 4: see pp. 131–2 below. In support, Hart points out that such radical divine transcendence was already established in principle, in the fourth century, when the doctrine of the Trinity was freed from subordinationism. It allowed us to conceive God no longer in relation to the world as the highest principle in a connected hierarchy of being, but as *sui generis* in his transcendence. Cf. also William Placher, *The Domestication of Transcendence* (Louisville, KY: Westminster John Knox Press, 1996).

Even so, Aquinas's overall schema undoubtedly remains significant. His concern to root providential purpose in the doctrine of God proved telling. His attempt to establish an undergirding doctrine of 'multiple' causality even more so. These are both fertile instincts, even if his formulation of them did not always satisfy. As indicated, they will surely need to be carried forward in some way.

Reformation concerns: Calvin and the sovereign will

The Reformation then naturally brought another set of developments. Many of the major changes here were only ecclesial: that is, changes to the sources of authority which purported to interpret the content of providence. This is not surprising. In a context of ecclesial controversy, the supposed content of providence would quickly become a ready weapon in power games, to be wielded on both sides of the divide to vindicate their position![38] But there were also some more formal doctrinal and conceptual shifts in the period, of the kind which currently concern us. In particular, an overall metaphysical dogmatism about divine being and sovereignty was replaced with a biblical dogmatism – and this led to a different order of conceptual concerns about providence.

Calvin especially became a key figure in this context, shifting his concerns to the substantive issues of biblical narrative rather than exploring the metaphysics of causality. Thus for him the paramount issue was to expound what he saw to be the overriding biblical witness to a sovereign divine will and purpose – and that is what made theological feathers fly in this period, more than any particular view of causality. It stirred theological controversy especially because Calvin developed this doctrine of divine sovereign will with such hard-edged determinism and divine predestination.[39] In his view, given the pre-eminence of God's will, this will must have its own way absolutely and implacably, in everything. This must be as true of events and people which appear to resist God's purpose as with those who align with it. In his own

---

[38] For a valuable survey of the effect of Protestant views of providence in 'ordinary' religion see Keith Thomas, *Religion and the Decline of Magic* (London: Weidenfeld and Nicholson, 1971), ch. 4.
[39] Calvin, *Institutes*, 1:16.4.

words: 'since the will of God is said to be the cause of all things, all the counsels and actions of men must be held to be governed by his providence; so that he not only exerts his power in the elect, who are guided by the Holy Spirit, but also forces the reprobate to do him service'.[40]

As with previous traditions, Calvin still wanted to distinguish this inexorable divine will from mere fate and Stoic philosophy. This was because Calvin also needed to fulfil another non-negotiable teaching of scripture; namely, that God is also just and free. And this means that God's will predestines everything not just for the sake of demonstrating absolute sovereignty per se, but also to demonstrate God's freedom to bring about just actions and outcomes. It means God's determination of everything, the end to which both 'elect' and 'reprobate' are guided, must always be displayed as a freely intended moral purpose, not blind fate. Calvin is explicit about this:

> Fate, named by the Stoics, is that which is necessary from the various and complicated labyrinth of causes that in some manner restricts God himself. By contrast with this, I define predestination, in line with what Holy Scripture teaches, as the free counsel of God by which he governs the human race and every single part of the universe according to his immense wisdom and incomprehensible justice.[41]

For the same reason, this overarching freedom of God to determine everything included some limited operation of human freedom. We are still free to intend any act within this will of God, even though God's will always has its way *through* our acts. That too distinguished this sort of theistic determination from the more impersonal Stoic forms of fate.

However, these distinctions and qualifications did not force any compromise into Calvin's view of divine sovereignty. As his disputations with the critic Castellio make especially clear, that sovereignty remains absolute. For whatever we intend and do we still cannot determine the meaning of the outcome – which belongs to God alone. A key example of this is emerges as Calvin tries to deal with the specific question of evil. If we commit evil, and if the will of God is the cause of all things, does that mean God wills the evil we do? Calvin's

---

[40] Ibid., 1:18.2.
[41] John Calvin, *The Secret Providence of God*, ed. Paul Helm (Wheaton, IL: Crossway, 2010), p. 62. The text is in the form of a series of disputations with an anonymous critic, whom he takes to be Sebastian Castellio.

answer, turning on this distinction between intention and act, is that God does not will our evil intentions but God does will all our acts, in so far as they can always made to serve God's ultimate (just) purpose.[42]

In similar vein, Calvin allows no significant distinction within our acts between those God wills and those God permits – because both will serve God's ultimate good purpose. The basis of this, following Augustine and Aquinas, is always God's sovereignty and omniscience (including foreknowledge).[43] Given this foreknowledge and 'highest authority' (i.e. sovereignty), it follows that God cannot have created any creature with the power to act against God's will (whatever the creature intends). That is why 'nothing happens unless he wills that it happens'.[44] Calvin's theological logic is remorseless here, and it is the nature of God's will as both sovereign and just which requires it. For it is always the integrity of God's will which provides the ultimate meaning in events, not any prior metaphysics of divine–human relations.

This last point is apparent in the brief references Calvin specifically makes to primary and secondary causality (what he calls 'remote' and 'immediate' causes). For this turns out to be less a metaphysical distinction and more a device just to allow him to distinguish human intention (which may be evil) from the overriding divine intention (good).[45] In other words, secondary causality appears not so much as a category to establish a significant distance between creator and creature, but only as another tool of the divine will – 'nothing but a modality of primary causality by which the sole determining cause of all events works out its positive decrees among creatures'.[46] So, again, it is precisely the all-sufficiency of divine will and purpose which is shaping the theology, not any prior metaphysics. It is the sovereign will which means secondary causality had to be subsumed as a modality within God's primary causality and human evil had to be subsumed within ultimate divine intention.

The implications of all this specifically for providence were broadly twofold. On the one hand this re-ordering of concerns certainly kept it high on the theological agenda. An absolutely paramount will of God, consistently affirmed

---

[42] Ibid., pp. 91–2.
[43] Ibid., pp. 75–6: 'If God foresaw what He did *not* will to be then He does not have the highest authority.'
[44] Ibid.
[45] Ibid., p. 101.
[46] Hart, *Providence and Causality*, p. 36.

even in the face of evil, naturally foregrounds providence. On the other hand, the insistence on God's absolute freedom and justice also, inevitably, renders it inscrutable. That is why Calvin talks readily of 'secret' providence; it is why he cites Job's failure to *see* God's justice at work until the very end; and it is why he appeals frequently to the conclusion of Paul's theology of history in Romans 9–11 where God's ways are 'unsearchable': 'oh the depth! [of the knowledge of God]' he cries, rhetorically.

As with other implications of predestination, this resort to secrecy has not necessarily convinced his critics – past or present. But overall his doctrine has still left an important legacy. In its very consistency about the sovereign divine will, this doctrine of providence has provoked creative reaction, especially in relation to the doctrine of God. After all, if we are not persuaded by secret meanings of providence, where else can we go except some trade-off between sovereignty and goodness in God? – something which Calvin's contemporary critics were quick to note (and later theologians even more so).[47] Such a collision between the reality of evil, human responsibility and a credible doctrine of a sovereign God, may not have been unique at this point. The sophistication of Aquinas's metaphysics of multiple causality was already one kind of response to this problem. But the issue was certainly sharpened here, in Calvin's hands.

Neither Aquinas nor Calvin themselves pursued its implications as radically as the reductionism of later modernity. That is to say, neither of them was willing to compromise divine sovereignty. For both of them the sovereign divine will remained paramount, in spite of these pressures to redefine it. Whether argued metaphysically (Aquinas) or scripturally (Calvin), divine sovereignty in all things simply would not be negotiated away. Nonetheless, just because they set the theological bar for sovereignty so high, the seeds of the challenge to it were effectively sown in this period. The challenge to providence itself then becomes clear: in what form can it persist, if at all, when pressures to reconceive fundamental aspects of the doctrine of God itself (including divine agency) become so telling?

---

[47] 'Castellio was perceptive in recognizing ... that between the theological outlook that he was representing and Calvin's views, there is a conflict between two conceptions of God. One is benign and universalistic in its intent but ultimately ineffectual; whereas the other is resolute in grace as well as in judgement ... always in control with ends that he unfailingly brings to pass'. Helm in Calvin, *The Secret Providence of God*, p. 19.

Modern shapes of providence: The travails of theological liberalism, from Schleiermacher to Wiles

This becomes even more apparent as we move on to the developments of modernity. These, of course, have been considerable. Every era generates some particular pressure to reconceive divine agency and providence – as we have seen, patristic and medieval theologies of sovereign divine purpose had to deal with the sacking of Rome and Arab philosophy; and Reformation theologies of providence had to operate in the face of ecclesial controversy and division. But, arguably, modern theology has had to deal with even more.

Most obviously, first, there was the rise of natural science. It has not been easy for theology to handle. By offering natural rather than metaphysical explanation for events, scientific thinking began to call into question any divine causation, in relation either to particular events or the cosmos as a whole. It re-opened the issue of causality but by sidelining metaphysics it also closed down the kind of revised notion of transcendent divine causality which might have rescued it.

There was also the rise of greater historical consciousness, especially in the nineteenth century. This issued the same sort of challenge to divine meaning in historical events as science did to natural events. By focusing attention empirically on the contingencies and relationalities of human agency and social conditions within historical process, the unfolding of events becomes self-interpreting – and the divine role becomes redundant. It pushes God back, if anywhere, to the remote regions of a transcendent but inert ground of events, just an impersonal deism – and that does not easily sustain anything like a full-blooded tradition of providence.

Unsurprisingly, many theological developments of providence in this period therefore became defensive and reductionist. There was, for example, the largely defensive reaction of Pietism and confessionalism. The theological energy here was only modest. Providence itself was not radically reconceived or re-imagined but simply asserted as part of its dogmatic heritage. There was no equivalent of Augustine's creativity when faced with an earlier form of historical consciousness.

One major theological figure attempted a more vigorous response. Friedrich Schleiermacher embraced notions of development and change in history more positively, and was concerned to relate these specifically to the providence of God.[48] Yet even here the response was modest in scope. The 'history' Schleiermacher was dealing with turns out to be largely the history of human consciousness, specifically religious consciousness, rather than natural or historical events as such. The main sphere left for providence was therefore reduced to an ethics of human action issuing from the religious consciousness. It was providential only in so far as it aligned itself with the (redemptive) will of God which has been grasped through that consciousness (supremely in Christ himself).

The celebrated theological critique of this offered later by Barth is that it subjectivized any significant *redemptive* action of God. The more fundamental criticism was its failure to really relate God to the world at all, in the actuality of either its natural or human history: that is, it only related God to human subjectivity (itself vulnerable to later reductionism from social and psychological sciences).[49] To be sure, a strand of Protestant liberal theology inspired by Schleiermacher remained influential, concentrating either on an unhistoricized dogmatic theology or treating history purely descriptively and scientifically: that is, as an entirely disenchanted backdrop to theology, rather than constitutive of it. But, as such, although it kept providence alive, it did so with only a very reduced sphere for divine action (and, arguably, an unsatisfactory doctrine of God).

Another limited response has been to draw on either Hegelian or process metaphysics, relating God to the world by embracing a more radical subjectivity and contingency within God's own being.[50] This provided a metaphysic in which God and world could relate more effectively in personal terms. But it has similar limitations. It has reduced the scope and effectiveness of divine action. Such metaphysics will not necessarily guarantee that the divine purposes can be fulfilled, not even eschatologically: a God of contingency easily becomes a vulnerable, risk-taking rather than sovereign God; a God imagined as agent

---

[48] In fact Schleiermacher prefers the notion of 'preservation' (*Erhlatung*) to the term 'providence' (*Vorsehung*), but this functions in his theology positively as a form of providence cf. F. D. E. Schleiermacher, *The Christian Faith* (Edinburgh: T & T Clark, 1928).

[49] Hodgson, *God in History*, pp. 24, 25: 'At the most fundamental level Schleiermacher's theology did not function with historical categories. ... The whole of dogmatics is ultimately derivable from "descriptions of human states of consciousness"...'.

[50] This does not mean either Hegelianism or process metaphysics need be adopted wholesale to develop this sort of doctrine God – but they are often background resources. Cf., for example, the discussions in Paul Fiddes, *The Creative Suffering of God* (Oxford: Clarendon Press, 1988).

without any radical difference to human being and action – and therefore inevitably limited. I will return to the Hegelian instincts which underlie this sort of theological response, because they have also operated more positively.[51] But their limiting effect must be acknowledged.

A similar outcome could also be seen in the response of much twentieth-century Anglo-Saxon analytical theology. This was a more targeted response to the scientific and historical critique of providence, and has created a very vigorous body of work about divine action. It was an attempt to re-express a doctrine of providence in terms of positivism, in accordance with rationalist canons of economy and coherence, and empirical support. Yet this too was often defensive and reductionist in outcome, strictly limiting the scope of divine action. Characteristically, it abandoned any notion of specific divine action or purpose in particular events.

Maurice Wiles exemplified this clearly.[52] He found it impossible to demonstrate special divine action empirically (for where can the supposed joint of divine causation actually be *seen* in events?). He also found it conceptually hard, if not impossible, to speak of special action without appeal to some form of unverifiable mysticism or metaphysics. So instead of trying to conceive particular divine acts Wiles conceived the world as a whole as a creative act of God. God is immanent in everything, but not causally active in any special way in any particular events. Where creatures actively respond to this pervading divine presence it may appear that a particular divine action and purpose is being carried out, but in fact the particularity is in our creaturely action, not in God's. It was an attempt to reinstate a form of the doctrine – but in very pared-down form. It turned out to be either another form of Schleiermacher's subjectivism or a re-formed deism (or, possibly, a kind of passive panentheism): that is, special divine action is really just a response of the human religious consciousness; distinctively divine 'action' itself is uniform, with special providence collapsed into general providence; and God is thereby reduced to an impersonal or passive reality.[53]

---

[51] See further below, pp. 93–4.
[52] Maurice Wiles, 'Religious Authority and Divine Action', in *Working Papers in Doctrine* (London: SCM Press, 1976), pp. 132–47; *God's Action in the World* (London: SCM Press, 1986).
[53] This assumes personhood is normally defined by the capacity for specific intentional agency, not just generalized 'presence'.

Moving beyond reductionism:
Personalism, idealism and Hegel

However, this is by no means the whole picture. There have been other trajectories of theology in this period, other kinds of response to modernity. In spite of the prevailing pressures towards deism, subjectivism or contingent theism, a less reductionist doctrine of God has also been maintained – along with a correspondingly robust doctrine of providence.

For example, within the analytical tradition, some philosophical theologians have been less shackled by extreme positivism. Brian Hebblethwaite and others, following Austin Farrer, have resisted the move to reduce theological meaning to empiricism. They have pointed out the category mistakes of any reductionist account which denies differentiations of divine causation solely on the grounds that this cannot be empirically mapped. Because divine causation is in a different category to others, its differentiated nature is not falsified by its empirical invisibility in the supposed 'causal joint' with creaturely agency.[54] This in turn has led to new accounts, drawn from the philosophy of action, offering conceptual possibilities of very specific purposive divine action at every level of human and natural reality.[55] God can readily be conceived to be actively realizing different purposes in different kinds of events without needing to demonstrate empirically any different kind of causation.

The driving force behind many of these accounts has been the integral nature of providence and a properly personalist doctrine of God. That is to say, they have assumed that any serious personal theism, in which knowledge of God as purposive agent is always bound up with personal interaction, must by definition be able to affirm a specific divine agency in the events of the world; for we only know personal reality through specificity and particularity.

This sort of rehabilitation of purposive divine agency in the analytic tradition has not always led to systematic doctrines of providence. But in other strands of modern theology this too has been revived. It has been strongly

[54] See, for example, Brian Hebblethwaite and Edward Henderson (eds), *Divine Action: Studies inspired by the Philosophical Theology of Austin Farrer* (Edinburgh: T&T Clark, 1990). See also critique of Wiles in Vernon White, *The Fall of a Sparrow: A Concept of Special Divine Action* (Exeter: Paternoster Press, 1985). This account is described as an invisible 'double-agency'.

[55] See, for example, White, *The Fall of a Sparrow*; also Thomas Tracey, *God, Action and Embodiment* (Grand Rapids: Eerdmans, 1984) and Thomas Tracey (ed.), *The God Who Acts: Theological and Philosophical Explorations* (Grand Rapids: Eerdmans, 1994).

reconfigured, for example, in some traditions of continental idealism (and, as we shall see, in neo-orthodoxy).

Thus in spite of its limitations noted earlier, some forms of Hegelianism have been fruitful. Their potential lay in Hegel's startling move to reconceive God *as* history – in the sense that history is the process through which God actually realizes God's own being ('without the world God is not God').[56] As we have seen, this could imply limitation to divine action. But for Hegel himself this wasn't entirely the case. He saw the process as dialectical in such a progressive sense that all movements and counter-movements of history could be construed as helping move it forward: that is, towards a final goal of realization. In that sense, God as history, not just in history, could effectively fulfil divine purposes.

This was an imaginative reconception of God, not least because it both drew on classical orthodoxy and subverted it at the same time. For example, it was trinitarian in so far as God's self-realization through time is constituted through incarnation and by the Spirit. But it was also more radically relational than classical trinitarianism because God's trinitarian relatedness is conceived to be mutually constitutive with the world (i.e. God's inner relatedness is also a relatedness to the world, rather than conceived solely in transcendental terms). Equally, it followed classical theism in so far as God's self-relatedness is logically prior to the world. But it also defied classical theism by conceiving God actualizing these relationships through the world (*pace* the doctrines of simplicity and aseity). As such this had great significance for providence. Such a God, after all, 'must' be working out purpose and progression through the events of history because that is how God actually constitutes God's own being.

Some serious difficulties still remain. Its underlying idealism is double-edged. Its dynamism gives momentum, but *too* inexorably. The Stoic-like necessity of this process of progressive realization can so easily became overwhelming, eliding history with God too closely and without 'remainder'. Also, in the interests of this historicization of progress, the individual too easily becomes subordinated to the final whole (a tendency also encountered in Spinoza). This set it at odds with foundational biblical and theological

---

[56] Hegel, *Lectures on the Philosophy of Religion*, 1:308n: usually reckoned to be a paraphrase by one of Hegel's editors.

axioms that God's purposes are revealed in the particular and individual, the proximate and 'marginal', not just in an overall final outcome: it failed to acknowledge theological pressure to find meaning *in*, not just through, the individual and particular.[57] As such it found itself at odds with Augustine's more nuanced (and biblical) vision of an unpredictable and less linear history. It left no room for God's eschatological purposes to supervene on ordinary empirical processes in relation both to the whole *and* the part. In short, it made too few concessions to the fact that history in itself is sometimes problematic rather than revealing.

This last point came to a head in the early years of the twentieth century against the background of devastating world war. This, for some, exposed more than ever before the poverty of any theology in which God is too closely elided with empirical human history (and its underlying subjective consciousness). It was the source of Barth's neo-orthodox critique of both Schleiermacher and Hegelian theology. In his view it was precisely that sort of elision which had blinded the German theological and intellectual establishment to the Kaiser's imperialistic war policy. Any theology which could support such gross evil must itself be grossly flawed. It must be constructing its notion of God's providential will and action on a merely immanent human edifice. It must have lost touch with any transcendent revelation for it to have so profoundly lost any critical distance from what was going on in actual history. When later the German Church also failed to distance itself (from Hitler), Barth attributed it to this same root cause: that is, a deficient theology of revelation, and a theology in which the being of God is simply elided with human history. In that sense this Hegelian theology, for all its promise, foundered on the very events which were supposed to support it.

Even so, Hegel's legacy still remains significant. The metaphysical straitjacket of classical theism was opened up. At least this allowed in principle much more radical re-imaginings of God's real relatedness to history and immanent divine activity within it. So whether or not it has satisfied in other respects, it has shifted the theological scenery significantly. More generally, it can at least be seen as another sign of the residual pressure of objective purpose: further

---

[57] Cf. Cyril O' Regan, 'Hegel, Theodicy and the Invisibility of Waste', in Murphy and Ziegler (eds), *The Providence of God*, pp. 75–108.

evidence of continued pressure to re-imagine providence constructively, not just reductively.

Barth's proposals (1): Transcendence and christocentricity

The more sustained counter to reductionism, however, came from neo-orthodoxy itself. So we also need to look at Barth's own positive proposals – which, I suggest, constitute the last really major waymark in this classical theological canon on providence, and arguably the most significant.

One reason for their significance – and controversial nature – is simply because of their very different starting point. Rather than adopting an all-embracing idealism in which God and the world are inseparable, Barth refused to import the imperfections of the world into the being of God. Instead, he began with a doctrine of God who radically transcends the world process.[58]

Prima facie this might seem counter-intuitive. It appears to sideline providence rather than foreground it. After all, a radical distinction between creator/creation means: 'God would be no less God even if the work of creation had never been, if there were no creatures, and if the whole doctrine of providence was therefore irrelevant.'[59] And at first sight Barth seems to confirm the downgrading of providence by locating it in his doctrine of creation, rather than a doctrine of God (*contra* Aquinas). Yet in fact it is precisely *as* radically transcendent that Barth's God can then be conceived to be effective as an agent within creation. This is extensively worked out in *Church Dogmatics* III/3, where it is the juxtaposition of these two theological concerns – the radical transcendence of God and a strong doctrine of divine overruling within human affairs – which generates his creativity about providence. The outcome is notable. When combined with Barth's rigorous christocentricity, a theology of providence emerges which reaffirms classic themes from pre-modernity, reacts to at least some issues of liberal modernity, yet also began to anticipate some re-imagining of postmodernity.

---

[58] Barth shared Hegelian instincts for a dynamic, relational, Trinitarian God, but his God was not constituted by such relations with the world. His God was relational, but transcendentally and self-sufficiently so, an irreducible mark of the *sui generis* nature of God *qua* God.

[59] Karl Barth, *Church Dogmatics* 111/3 (Edinburgh: T & T Clark, 1976), p. 36.

How is this worked out? It is expressed dogmatically first: that is as an expression of its location in the doctrine of creation. Here, contrary to what we might expect, providence is far from short-changed. Instead it is described comprehensively as the 'continuation and history' of what is given in the general order of creation by a process of 'preservation, accompaniment and rule' (*conservation, concursus, gubernatio*).[60] Moreover, although formally distinguished from the covenant history of redemption, its dogmatic exposition ultimately includes this too. Providence emerges as the overall generic river of God's whole activity in history (the history of the covenant flowing just as one current within it). This is a metanarrative of the *whole* of history; all historical events are subject to divine purposive activity in some sense. It is, therefore, as universal in scope and uncompromising in its expression of divine sovereignty as for Calvin. In Barth's terms, God's purposive rule is a 'universal lordship' which is 'the basis and meaning' of all creaturely history.[61]

Admittedly, the basis for all this is fideistic. That is to say, it follows from the revelation of God in Christ through the scriptures, received within creaturely existence through faith – rather than through any independent source of reason or empirically based natural theology. This was the basis for all Barth's theology; it was not supported by any kind of independent reason, or metaphysics, to explain *how* this divine and human (or natural) agency might work together, or how the being and act of God might be conceived in this relation. Nor did it attempt to relate explicitly to scientific discourse and accommodate its terms accordingly. In this sense Barth was an heir to a reformed dogmatic tradition more than any other, and it might seem simply a reversion to Pietism or confessionalism. It seems to lack any direct attempt to engage with modernity, inductive historicism and the authority of reason.

However there is re-framing of at least some of these issues in Barth which suggests otherwise. This shows that he *is* engaging post-critically, not just in a pre-modern way. For example, Barth collapses the traditional Reformed distinction between general and special providence (*providentia ordinaria* and *providentia extraordinary*). This makes it clear he is not relying on any naive

---

[60] Barth, CD 111/3, p. 8. Note, however, that this location does not necessarily imply the conflation of creation and history. For the importance of maintaining this distinction see Oliver O'Donovan, *Resurrection and Moral Order* (Leicester: Apollos, 2nd ed. 1994). Creation is the condition of history, so not subsumed entirely as the teleology and process of history (just as eschatology is not simply subsumed into that process).

[61] Barth, CD 111/3, p. 239.

pre-modern account of God's 'direct' intervention, nor is he needing any other kind of empirical distinction between God's activity in natural regularities and elsewhere. Instead, God's activity by Barth's definition transcends all these distinctions anyway – which is precisely what pre-empts the critiques of the empiricists and the Humean challenge about miracles.

This appeal to transcendence does not mean Barth rules out God's capacity to have particular purposes in particular creaturely events (he is no crypto deist). Nor does it imply a doctrine of impersonal uniformity of divine will and action (he is no Wilesian). On the contrary, Barth's treatment of all divine causality as uniquely transcendent is precisely the reason why he *can* affirm special divine purpose in particular events[62] – but he can now affirm all this in a way that bypasses the Humean critique. Admittedly, this is still unashamedly dogmatic and confessional in the sense that this metaphysical account of divine causality and purpose derives ultimately from faith's perception of reality, not scientific or historical observation.[63] Even so, this re-framing is clearly accommodating a scientific empiricism rather than simply denying it.

More generally Barth also re-frames, rather than ignores, the issue of how we can have any knowledge of God and the being of God. For by describing God throughout in christological and trinitarian terms he is effectively adopting a personalist philosophy. That is, he is assuming all revealed knowledge of God is received primarily through personal relation, rather than through abstract or detached reasoning on 'objective' empirical reality.[64] This may not satisfy a rationalist or positivist epistemology (arguably, it is recasting the *sui generis* being and agency of God more in postmodern terms). But it at least offers some alternative determinative framework, rather than nothing. He is re-framing not ignoring the challenge.

Barth's most substantive re-framing, however, comes with his new kind of focus on narrative and history. He insists that history, together with its narrative form, is the primary place where the theologian must look for (divine) meaning

---

[62] Barth, *CD* 111/3, pp. 160–5.

[63] As John Webster has put it, the meaning of causation follows from what faith perceived in providential history, rather than explaining it: 'the metaphysics follows the confession which it explicates'. Webster, 'On the Theology of Providence', p. 168. Webster is not explicitly quoting Barth here, but it is an apt description of his theological method.

[64] Not all would see Barth as naturally personalist. He was reticent about person language in some contexts, and certainly wary of all 'isms'. Nonetheless his theism clearly expounds ultimate reality as relational, dynamic and personal. Cf. discussion in Darren M. Kennedy, *Providence and Personalism* (Oxford: Peter Lang, 2011).

and purpose. So in that sense he engages fully with modernist historical consciousness. He can do this because he focusses the reading of history through the lens of christocentric faith, rather than through positivism. He offers a reading of history through the particular narrative of Christ. In other words, he insists that the hermeneutical centre of all history, and therefore the purpose of all history, is founded uniquely in the particular narrative of Jesus Christ. This christocentric reading is not an arbitrary lens because it is in the Christ narrative that the personal revelation of faith is empirically founded; but it is a very particular lens (and in that sense, again, more an anticipation of postmodernity).

Such radical christocentricity is not just an abstract point of methodology. It also re-frames the whole of his theology substantively. It determines, for example, the meaning of divine sovereignty. It means that the nature of God's power and purpose in ordering and overruling all things is always Christ-shaped: that is, it is not derived from some abstract notion of 'absolute power', but from the way God particularly and concretely exercised his power and carried out his purpose in Christ. It also determines any possible attempt at theodicy. Although Barth himself did not follow this through fully, a Christ-shaped and cruciform account of divine activity provides the only possible meaning in God's relation to evil.[65]

Even more germane is its implication specifically for providence. Here it is particularly creative. It helps re-frame providence as a bridge between the particular and universal. For as a particular narrative itself, chistocentricity affirms the meaning of all particulars; yet the meaning it secures for them is also, through the cosmic Christ, a relation to history as a whole.[66] *Contra* Hegel, it therefore secures the value of particular lives and narratives in the purposes of God as particular creaturely realities, not just as instances of general principles – yet without abandoning the sense of metanarrative as well.

It is hard to overestimate the importance of this principle for Barth. To see particular history both as a locus of meaning and value in itself and in relation to a whole, is all of a piece with locating providence within creation. After all,

---

[65] Cf. Gorringe, *God's Theatre*. Gorringe finds Barth's acknowledgement of the paradoxical nature of the way divine power is exercised in a cruciform way only fully realized in his doctrine of reconciliation, after he had completed his account of providence.

[66] Barth, *CD* 111/3, p. 183: 'In [these] *particular* events ... the rule of God has the centre which controls and is normative for everything else' [emphasis mine].

creation itself is always limited, finite, particular, as well as 'universal'. This is how and why creation can be loved; divine love (creative and redemptive) only means anything if it has specific and particular realities as its objects of action, as well as the enterprise as a whole.[67] Thus the particularity of providence, as of creation, secures it as always an act of love.

It is also all of a piece with Barth's eschatology. For when the time comes when history can 'progress no further', 'everything that has happened in the course of that history will then take place as a recapitulation together of *all individual events*', such that every particular creature can retain an 'eternal existence'.[68] Here both the universality and the radical particularity of the narrative is especially clear: all these individual events of creation gain their full meaning both by being 'recapitulated together', and by being valued in themselves – through the Christ event which is the means by which this redemption and recapitulation occurs. Thus the point is always twofold: a universal story of Christ is being told, but it is only constituted through the value of the particular as well.[69]

There are, naturally, some critical questions to be asked. What is the 'meta' relation between the pivotal narrative of Christ and other particular sub-narratives? If their meaning and purpose is ultimately secured only by Christ's narrative, can they have any real integrity in their own history? And if the various sub-narratives of history all ultimately connect to Christ, must they not also connect to each other in one overall stream? In other words, this might still seem a metanarrative which flattens different stories into one in the end, not so different from Hegelianism after all.

Barth would certainly resist this – not least because of this insistence that, in Christ, particularities are so fully endorsed. When Christ himself is the metanarrative, the metanarrative is itself being constituted by particularity

---

[67] Barth, *CD* 111/3, p. 7. 'The Creator-God of the Bible is not a world-principle developing in an infinite series of productions … His creative activity has a limit appointed by Himself and His Love in the fact that He is content with His creature as a definite and limited object and has addressed Himself only but totally to it as such'. However, this sense of limit doesn't mean that Barth denies change and new occurrences (provided this is seen as a divine activity, not only a natural process) cf. *CD* 111/3, p. 56.

[68] Barth, *CD* 111/3, pp. 87–8 (emphasis mine).

[69] Cf. also Barth, *CD* 111/3, pp. 167–8: 'In determining creaturely activity and its effects, God directs it to a common goal, that is Himself. But this does not mean that particular creatures, individuals and historical groupings and relationships are prevented by Him from existing in their particularity and for particular ends. Nor does it mean that … the endless variety of happenings which go to make up world history as a whole will later be ironed out and destroyed in favour of a … unified plan'.

so in principle particularity cannot be supressed.[70] How this actually works, however, does now need more attention.

Barth (2): A figural outline of providence – and its apophaticism

Perhaps the best way to describe how Barth can sustain this is to distinguish between linear and figural relations between events.[71] The purposes of God are not necessarily worked out through a linear trajectory in which all sequences of events fit a causal chain towards a single overarching end. Instead, they are co-ordinated as they exist in the integrity of their own separate sequences in figural relation to a more complex overall end which is 'Himself' (i.e. Himself in the Christ event).[72] This figural relation may be defined as a family resemblance with other events which does not require direct spatial, causal or temporal connection, but may be a-temporal or synchronic (i.e. it is the kind of relation referred to previously, for example, between the meaning of a piece of music and an experience of love, or between political events in different geo-political spheres).[73]

Barth demonstrates this primarily through exegesis. Exegesis uncovers this 'historical multiformity' which 'cannot be reduced to a formula', yet it is all still ultimately related to 'the name of Jesus Christ'.[74] This is clearest in his discussion of election where he describes 'types' of biblical figures – in all of whom we recognize the electing work of Christ, but 'not in exactly the same way', nor by necessary causal link. As such, these figural relations are for Barth the characteristic way in which this sort of providence can be perceived. They are the way particulars can be seen to relate to a wider purpose, but without losing their integrity. They are the way we see providence in many smaller stories, even when we cannot see the way it is joined up in one bigger story.

---

[70] Barth's overall assertion that particularity is *integral* to the metanarrative, is particularly fertile. It is picked up later in Quash, *Found Theology*. See further below pp. 105–6.

[71] 'Figural' reading, in some form is not new to Barth, of course. He appropriated it from older sources. They can be traced back in some form back to Origen. Cf. John Dawson, *Christian Figural Reading and the Fashioning of Identity* (Berkeley: University of California Press, 2002).

[72] See note 69 above: 'God directs ... to a common goal, that is Himself'.

[73] See p. 27 above.

[74] Karl Barth, *Church Dogmatics 11/2* (Edinburgh: T& T Clark, 1957), p. 366.

Such figural relations mean that this providence will not be easily perceived. It will only be grasped through faith, not by independent empirical observation or deduction. In fact even with faith Barth thinks that the Christian is still going to be perplexed: 'he is faced every day afresh with the riddles of the world-process, with the precipices and plains, the blinding lights and obscurities, of the general creaturely occurrence to which his own life's history also belongs.'[75] God laughs at our attempts to see His rule, Barth says earlier, and only 'one day', that is, eschatologically, will we will be able to see how God is Lord both of the general and the particular.

As such the overall metanarrative of this figural connections is certainly not luminous – and a degree of apophaticism about specific instances of providence will always be appropriate. But then this is not, on many views, a weakness. It is a strength. For it is precisely why such an account of providence cannot easily be conceptually, morally or politically instrumentalized into oppression.[76]

Here too there may be questions. A bare assertion of meaning and purpose in events, without interpretation in particular cases, is unlikely to satisfy all. Arguably it exposes a failure of nerve. It might also seem like an internal contradiction because Barth's generally strong focus on particulars in principle is not carried through consistently here; as Frei has complained, Barth is so indeterminate about particular interpretation that he is open to the charge of idealization after all.[77] Another complaint is Barth's reluctance to spell out the metaphysical framework necessary to support the kind of divine action which constitutes these (hidden) figural relations, just as he does not elaborate the concept of transcendent causality itself (in spite of using the term 'causality').[78]

Nonetheless, overall it remains a *tour de force*. If nothing else its sheer dominance and vitality in Barth's own structure of thinking is simply further testimony to the doctrine's resilience. But more than that, there are these creative moves he has made. The re-framing of causality and the implicit use

[75] Barth, *CD 111/3*, p. 242.
[76] Cf. John Webster, 'The Grand Narrative of Jesus Christ: Barth's Christology', in G. Thompson and C. Moster (eds), *Karl Barth: A Future for Postmodern Theology?* (Hindmarsh: Australian Theological Forum, 2000), pp. 29–48.
[77] Hans Frei, in Paul Ramsey (ed.), *Faith and Ethics* (New York: Harper & Row, 1957). Frei was also concerned that Barth's insistence on historical particularity did not even attend much to the empirical details of Christ's own life, especially in the early part of the *Dogmatics*.
[78] Cf. Kennedy's critique in *Providence and Personalism*, pp. 229, 313.

of personalist philosophy is significant. For Barth at least, it accommodates positivist challenges without reductionism. Even more important, there are his christological and figural readings of narrative. These are fertile and new trajectories.[79] As we shall see, they will prove a ready basis for new imaginings of providence – especially as it enters postmodernity.

Frei, Hodgson, Hardy: Narrative, postmodern and postliberal theologies

Before we turn to new imaginings, however, just two further waymarks to note which will help complete this initial mapping: the first, an extension of Barth's concern for figural narrative which we find in Hans Frei (of whom more in the next chapter); the second, more generally, the connection we then also see between this figural trajectory and postmodern/ postliberal concerns.

First, Frei should be noted because he pursued a narrative reading in a more systematic and intentional way. Worried by what he saw as an 'eclipse' of narrative in the eighteenth century, and believing narrative flow essential to convey meaning (including providential meaning), he made it his priority to reinstate it for theology in the same way it had been rediscovered in social and moral philosophy.[80] In particular, he explicitly foregrounded the 'history-like' nature of biblical narrative, specifically to establish its role in displaying the identity of Christ in providence – which, as for Barth, was to be figurally understood. He saw this as vital for displaying it as a publicly accessible theology. What he produced was therefore a compelling analysis which traced the story of how (figural) narrative was eclipsed, and which made the case for reinvigorating it.[81]

This was not unproblematic. Frei was so convinced by the significance of specifically historical narrative that its revelatory transcendence may have been too muted. Put another way, his insistence that he had to operate as a historian

---

[79] See note 77 above – figural reading itself is not wholly new in Barth, though his development of it surely was.

[80] Hans Frei, *The Eclipse of Biblical Narrative: A Study in Eighteenth and Nineteenth Century Hermeneutics* (New Haven: Yale University Press, 1974); *The Identity of Jesus Christ* (Philadelphia: Fortress Press, 1975).

[81] Frei thought that the modern process of historicization, which should have required close attention to narrative, actually bypassed narrative because of its quest for assured truths of reason. So

may have reduced his effectiveness as a theologian – I shall return to that later. Nonetheless, his overall focus undoubtedly reinforced the fundamental turn taken by Barth. It should certainly be noted as part of this classical canon we are tracking.

Then, second, we should note the connections of these narrative readings with postmodern and postliberal developments. Postmodernity generally has consistently looked to find meaning in displaced or non-linear narratives and particular configurations within narrative – an inevitable consequence of their wariness with the way reason and power have exploited 'ordinary' metanarrative. Hence Foucault's attenuated sense of history as 'the difference of times'; Derrida's designation of history as 'labyrinth'; and Lyotard's seminal essay on the demise of the grand narrative. These all demonstrate in different ways that linear readings of history are problematic, particularity matters, and meaning must therefore be sought in other ways than the linear.[82]

Figural theology after Barth and Frei naturally relates to this. Their conception of providence includes just this acknowledgement that all histories have particularities which cannot be flattened into one linear trajectory. Their stock-in-trade has been precisely a concentration on unique meaning in the figural particularities of history (pivotally, in Christ himself), rather than any ideologically imposed pattern.

To be sure, this connection too is by no means unproblematic. The deconstruction of more extreme postmodernism admits no possibility of any providential meaning at all, not even figurally. It will dismiss all events just as 'an eternally fooling, maddening, clowning, jesting tricking … field of force'.[83] Here there simply is no such thing at all as history with objective meaning and purposes: there are only disparate events, which we might choose to group in certain ways but which carry no compelling reason or pattern within themselves. It is like a return to a pre-modern world as merely playground for

---

'somewhere around the eighteenth century' the narrative of the Bible became read less in its own terms and its own narrative integrity. Instead it was excavated for 'what really happened' and for its eternal underlying truths which could then apply to us all. This denied it the narrative flow which Frei considered so essential. Specifically, it sidelined the chief source of providential meaning, which is the identity of Jesus Christ. He is conveyed pre-eminently in narrative, and conveys providential meaning in that form: so when narrative itself is bypassed, so too is this vital Christological source of meaning. Cf. Mike Higton's illuminating discussion in *Christ, Providence and History: Hans W Frei's Public Theology* (Edinburgh: T & T Clark, 2004), especially ch. 2.

[82] Cf. especially J.-F. Lyotard, *The Postmodern Condition: A Report of Knowledge* (Minneapolis: University of Minnesota Press, 1984).

[83] Mark Taylor, *Erring: a Postmodern Theology* (Chicago: University of Chicago Press, 1984).

capricious gods – except they are now not even gods, just random forces. In this whirling void of events we may try to shape things as best we can but there is no overall guiding shape 'out there' to work towards. This radical postmodernism obviously takes us a very long way from Barth or Frei with their theology of history – in which there *is* still a definite and purposive narrative to be found, rooted in the will of a personal God, even though we have no 'master-key' to unlock it.[84]

Yet, these extremes apart, a figural approach can connect generally with the particularity of this post-modern temper, and remain genuinely theological. So, for example, Peter Hodgson's *God in History* is a sustained exploration of a theology of history in which events are honoured in their separate integrity, yet still ultimately interrelated in God. He develops this in different ways to Barth. He identifies the signs of providence not just in the load-bearing events of scripture but in all events which are 'foci of creativity': that is, events which are self-evidently generative of freedom, or justice, or love.[85] He also foregrounds the shaping role of an inspired human praxis. This means that the involvement of the human self with story-making, central to so much late-modern thinking, is more evident, and the notion of objective divine agency less so. Indeed, Hodgson is reluctant to describe God at all as shaping events like 'an agent performing acts'. Yet he is still representing God as a determinative presence, as an indwelling Spirit who acts by disclosing and being the 'normative' shape of this process of praxis.[86] Moreover, it is an effective divine action with wide scope, because these apparently disparate events of praxis are so inspired in this way that they can ultimately bring about some sort of metanarrative, a 'creative unification of multiplicities of elements'.[87]

Overall this may be more Hegelian than Barthian – and whether it is an adequate account of Christian providence is arguable.[88] Yet it is by no means a wholly reductionist or subjectivist account. And it clearly takes inspiration from Barth's main overall concerns. That is to say, it is trying to do justice

---

[84] Cf. Barth, *CD* 111/3, p. 242.
[85] W. A. Beardslee's phrase: 'Christ in the Postmodern Age', in D. R. Griffin (ed.), *Varieties of Postmodern Theology* (Albany: State University of New York Press, 1989), pp. 63–80.
[86] Hodgson, *God in History*, p. 205.
[87] Ibid.
[88] See further pp. 125–40 below, on the importance of maintaining transcendence.

to these two major themes of theology which stand in tension but refuse to give way to each other: namely, the meaning that inheres in particular events which cannot be forced easily into an overall pattern – and the pervasive sense that there is an overall meaning and purpose nonetheless, however opaque. So this too should be noted as another marker to the resilience of the tradition.

Similarly, we should also note the later more English (certainly Anglican) strand of postliberal theology represented by such figures as Dan Hardy and Ben Quash. This is not a body of work with a particular focus on providence as such. Much of it is concerned about a particular way of doing theology rather than the exposition of any particular substantive doctrine. Yet as Hardy, Quash and others in this tradition pursue their methodology, an underlying development of a doctrine of providence is clearly evident – one which again offers an example of a general fit between figural and late-modern concerns.

Hardy's methodology, for example, requires special attentiveness to ecclesial performances in a way which immediately suggests robust providential patterns.[89] For when Hardy looks at the performance of the eucharist what he sees is a specific exemplification of a more general relationship between God and human reality which is dynamic, transformative and purposive. The purposiveness displayed there is extensive and objective precisely because it is sacramental. That is, it is embedded in all material realities (biological, social, political, cultural), and it is not just a function of individual subjectivity. The same providential meaning is apparent in Hardy's attention more generally to empirical particularities. For what he sees in these particularities (like Coleridge) is not just the thing 'in itself' but also a *telos*, a 'tending towards' something greater. In short, what he sees is that things are only 'formed in their fullness' by reference also to 'the purposes of God'.[90]

For Quash, likewise, methodological commitment is inseparable from some sort of providential framework. Quash too deals with particularity. He is especially concerned with the particular historical nature of our theological

---

[89] Cf. Daniel Hardy, *Finding the Church: The Dynamic Truth of Anglicanism* (London: SCM Press, 2001).

[90] Cf. Daniel Hardy, 'Harmony and Mutual Implication in the *Opus Maximum*', in J. W. Barbeau (ed.), *Coleridge's Assertion of Religion: Essays on the Opus Maximum* (Leuven: Peeters, 2006), pp. 33–52. Cited in Quash, *Found Theology*.

knowledge, in which we gain insight through historical process – specifically, for Quash, as it emerges via analogical reasoning in the interplay between the 'given' insights of scripture and tradition and newly 'found' insights occasioned by particular and contingent historical circumstances.[91] And, vitally, this is not random: for he is also relying on a 'certain ontology of the historical process' in which God (*qua* Holy Spirit) has '*placed*' these things to be found.[92] In other words it implies, as with Barth, that these particular found things are honoured in their particularity not over against any overall metanarrative but integrally to it – precisely because they are 'placed' 'gathered', 'related' by the Spirit.[93]

Quash also employs a specifically figural approach to reinforce this providential meaning of things. Using found art as an analogy (where there is also an 'unbidden conjunction' of things), 'a divinely ordained patterning of history' may arise through discerning unusual juxtapositions, not necessarily through the normal temporal or casual links of linear history.[94]

As with Hodgson, Barth clearly lies behind these contributions. His recovery of narrative and figural reading is a common theme. There is also a good deal of critical development of Barth. They part company with him in theological method and epistemology (critiquing him for his failure to see history sufficiently as a site for *growth* in knowledge, and his tendency to impose purpose on history rather than encounter it within history). They also move well beyond Barth through their more developed pneumatology (especially Quash). This helps draw attention to the dynamic interpenetration of God and reality.

But what is constant in this development is again the persistence of providence, and in a fairly robust form. These postliberal theologies may not foreground it in systematic terms as an abstracted doctrine in its own right, yet it remains on their agenda. And as such they bring this continuing tradition of providential thinking right up to the present.

---

[91] See Quash, *Found Theology*.

[92] Ibid., pp. 15, 138.

[93] Ibid., p. 276: 'The Spirit works particularly, making things more what they are, concretizing them rather than homogenizing them. ... But the Spirit also gathers and relates things more intensively than any ingenious human scheme – whether of thought or action – could do on its own. The radical particularization by the Spirit is not atomization (the multiplication of arbitrary units) but generates the basis of communion.'

[94] Ibid., pp. 3, 112. Thus, for example, Job can be retrieved and put alongside a Carpaccio painting to show some meaning in suffering.

An agenda to carry forward

Such, then, are some of the roots and developments of this core belief. It is a fertile tradition which continues to seek God's meaning and action in all kinds of events, in particulars as well as overall outcomes. It is a specifically theological account of interconnecting purpose in all things, incorporating our own purposes but not reducing to them. It has consistently framed the purpose we experience as the dynamic will of a personal God who is a radically transcendent agency, not competing with our own but fulfilling it. It does not necessarily identify the meaning of all particular events but it does affirm they can all bear meaning, if only figurally. And it is a resilient tradition. In spite of all the countervailing pressures of creaturely contingency, autonomy, the reality of evil, the experience of the surd, it persists. Indeed, new chapters are still being added.[95]

To be sure, these waymarks of the tradition which I have noted are selective. They do not tell the whole story, nor do they tell it in the only way possible: there are other theologies of a more radically vulnerable God not fully explored here. Nor have they answered all questions. Issues of causality and metaphysics have not all been settled. The reality of evil and suffering still needs more recognition. The changing sense of self as an interactive and responsive agent needs taking more fully into account. The actual empirical shape and identification of (purported) non-linear meanings may need more defence. For all these reasons more imaginings of this providence are surely needed, as the next chapter will acknowledge.

Even so, the weight and resilience of this 'classic' canon still has to be reckoned with. It is a basis which cannot lightly be dismissed – whatever new shapes may also be required.

---

[95] In addition to some of the more obvious postliberal developments there are others which could also be pursued. Tim Gorringe's brief review of analogies in his theology of providence (*God's Theatre*) provides examples of an almost endlessly fertile field. Not least his own analogy. Drawing on the improvising experience of Peter Brook, a former Director of the Royal Shakespeare Company, Gorringe projects onto God a similar reticence to impose any complete 'scheme' or 'plan'. Divine purpose proceeds best, suggests Gorringe, like a creative and improvised direction of a play (with God as both director and co-actor). As an analogy this raises many of the same issues that have emerged before: the nature of causality, the limits of autonomy, the relation of sub-narratives to the plot as a whole, whether and how the 'overall' sense of the play can be sovereignly secured. It does not resolve them. But it is a creative way of keeping unresolved issues in play together – and offers yet another example of the continuing resilience of the doctrine. The notion of improvisation is effectively developed more systematically as a theological category by, for example, Sam Wells in *Improvisation: The Drama of Theological Ethics* (London: SPCK, 2004).

4

Some Theological Re-imaginings

When turning to new imaginings of providence, one obvious pressure to be dealt with has to do with conceptual credibility. As we have seen, the attempt to find appropriate concepts of divine causality to sustain transcendent meaning in an overall metanarrative of events has been a recurring issue throughout much of the doctrine's history. It is always a challenge to find concepts which can command credibility within shifting critical frameworks of thought. So this necessarily sets part of the agenda. Further theological re-imagining must at the very least take this into account, even if it cannot wholly resolve it.

But even more momentum to reconfigure comes from empirical issues: that is, from the pressure of events themselves. These always lie in the background of theological history, whether or not named and acknowledged. New events and the continuing aftershock of past events will always challenge providence and demand new imaginings of it, especially when they involve great evil. Such events as the Lisbon earthquake of 1755 and more recently the Holocaust of the 1940s produced a seismic shock, both literal and metaphorical, which tears at any shape we construct to 'explain' them.

The earthquake's wanton and wide-scale destruction in Lisbon on All Saints Day offered a particularly powerful example. It shook all firm footings for transcendent meaning and purpose. It called into question even the philosophical securities that Descartes thought he had found.[1] It specifically prompted Voltaire to reject any providential view of the world; Leibniz's notion that all was for the best in 'the best of all possible worlds' simply seemed unsustainable in the light of this irruption of natural evil.[2] The human evil of the Nazi Holocaust nearly 200 years later had a similar widespread effect.

---

[1] Cf. Werner Hamacher, 'The Quaking of Presentation', in *Premises: Essays on Philosophy and Literature from Kant to Celan* (Redwood City: Stanford University Press, 1999), pp. 261–93.

[2] Voltaire, *Poème sur le désastre de Lisbonne.*

Moreover, while Lisbon, the Holocaust, the 2003 Tsunami, are the large-scale headlines of such events, every single individual personal tragedy counts just as much. The raw experience of all these sorts of events combines with the shifts in conceptual and critical thought, and acts cumulatively. It is part of wider transformation of European culture and philosophy that Theodor Adorno and others describe.

Both conceptual and empirical challenges to transcendent purpose therefore keep pressing – and what follows will try to take some account of both kinds of pressures. The previous chapter began the process. This chapter must now dig deeper. First by dealing with the conceptual issues: how the bare conceivability of divinely steered events might be rethought. Then by dealing more with the empirical issues: how the overall shape of God's story might accommodate actual events when they are so baffling. Finally, we shall need to look again at notions of transcendence which, I shall suggest, underlie all these new imaginings.

In the course of this I make no claim to any major area of originality. Much of this is a critical review of other contributions, or just a new perspective on them. But, as such, it is at least an attempt to make sure these discussions continue – and to ensure they do so constructively, not just reductively.

Conceptual issues: Imagining divine agency and the causal joint

I begin with the notion of divine agency itself, and specifically causality – one of the most regularly re-examined of the conceptual issues. If events bear God's meaning, not just ours, then God is acting in them, but how can this be conceived? As our understanding of empirical processes of causation has increased so too has the pressure to clarify divine causality. Can there be any significant re-imagining here?

One strategy could be just to kick this into touch. We could reject the terms of the question. Instead, we could see semiology as a replacement for all these hard questions about causality.[3] Recognizing the reality of sign-making is,

---

[3] Rowan Williams sometimes seems to come close to this: see for example Williams, 'Language, Reality and Desire in Augustine's *De Doctrina*'.

at root, the suggestion that events can always convey another transcendent meaning while retaining their own empirical integrity.[4] This could make all questions about causality redundant; for if we can identify events in the world which have, as a matter of fact, re-ordered meaning for us, then we identify God's activity and purpose without needing any particular theory of causality. The underlying appeal here is to a radical category of transcendence in which divine action does not compete at all with causation, and so there is no need to show how they relate. A good deal of theology does in fact operate like this now, and I believe this appeal to radical transcendence does ultimately have to be made (and I will return to it).

However I do not want simply to close down all questions of causality so swiftly. For there has also been some more direct theological engagement with causality, which has opened up more imaginative and conceptual space around the issue even if it does not resolve it. This too tends to depend ultimately on a notion of radical transcendence, but only after some sort of real engagement with other more accessible discourse.

In fact there has been a spectrum of approaches here. At one end of the spectrum the direct engagement with empirical sciences is, admittedly, very small. At the other it is more considerable. But all show some creative attempt, from within a post-Enlightenment world, to relate creaturely causality to divine agency and divine causality. Moreover, when these approaches are combined with new models some new constructive theology is always possible. So in what follows I will briefly review all these. This means, first, recapitulating two of these approaches already touched on in the previous mapping. I then review another kind of approach not previously mentioned. Finally, I will offer a more extended discussion of an attempt to combine them all.

A spectrum of theological approaches

First, we should recall that approach to causality taken by dogmatic theology. This lay at one end of the spectrum, in one sense hardly engaging at all with empirical causality. As we saw with Barth's neo-orthodoxy, the appeal here was to a notion of divine causality as wholly other: that is, not derived from

---

[4] Cf. Rowan Williams, 'The Nature of a Sacrament', in *On Christian Theology* (Oxford: Blackwell, 2000), p. 207, where he applies this to sacramental theology.

empirical observation nor from any wider metaphysics of causality but from faith and revelation. This foregrounds divine agency and purpose, and even uses the language of causality, but always insists that other empirical accounts of causality can only accompany, rather than determine, the meaning of this divine causality.

Prima facie this might seem to short-change the question of causality in much the same way as an appeal to signs. It is a refusal to examine its relation to creaturely causality in any other terms than revelation. It also implies a metaphysical basis to this relation which is largely unexplored.[5] Yet as we also saw, it does not deny these other accounts outright. It is still deliberately allowing the two kinds of account stand alongside each other. In that sense it is at least an acknowledgement of the integrity of other meanings of causality, even if it does not directly engage with them. Moreover, as such, it allows space for some of the theological paradoxes of providence in a way that the attempt to translate between the two accounts may not. It allows active divine sovereign presence and real creaturely agency to co-exist without conflict and competition – and this capacity to retain theological paradox without compromise is notable.[6]

Second, we should also recall the approach taken by analytical theology. This lay further along the spectrum. It has tried to establish the meaning of personal and divine agency in precisely those positivist terms which dogmatic theology largely disdained.[7] Admittedly, much of this ends up reductionist (as we saw with Wiles); it is not easy to formulate ideas of an effective personal but non-bodily agency within a strictly empirical or logical frame of reference. Yet if tight positivist rules are relaxed just enough to allow a little more reference range to meaning and language, the approach can generate some more constructive accounts. There are some defensible conceptions of purposive non-bodily divine agency. As noted, a higher form of causality can be conceived to incorporate a lower in a form of 'double agency' in which specific divine purposes are realized through different events even though there may be no differentiated causal mode visible.[8] Again, there are limitations: this sort of

---

[5]   Cf. Kennedy, *Providence and Personalism*. This is an attempt to locate Barth more intentionally in personalist philosophy, though not in any wider metaphysic.

[6]   Cf. John Webster, *Barth's Moral Theology: Human Action in Barth's Thought* (Edinburgh: T & T Clark, 1998).

[7]   See pp. 91–2 above.

[8]   Ibid., p. 92, note 54.

approach still has not engaged directly with the causal joint in strictly scientific terms; the joint is left as an intrinsically opaque point of contact which is causal only analogically or transcendentally. Even so, some more traction has been gained here. There is at least some more precision in what we *mean* by divine agency in such notions of double agency – and this too is notable.

Next, there is this other approach not previously mentioned. This lies still further along the spectrum. It is the kind of natural theology which derives specifically from a dialogue between science and theology, and which quite clearly engages directly with empirical science. In its earlier forms this was not always convincing because it tended to look for the point of purchase of divine agency and causation in gaps in the scientific causal story – and gaps, of course, have a habit of closing over when new scientific accounts emerge. It has also tended to be theologically reductionist. As Aquinas noted long before, a God who only acts in the absence of other causes is an inadequate concept of God as well as a vulnerable concept of causality. However, more recent natural theology prompted by new scientific perspectives has been more promising. Scientist-theologians such as John Polkinghorne and Arthur Peacocke have drawn on various aspects of indeterminacy in the natural world to offer other sophisticated models of divine action which do not rely on any kind of gap in a causal story, nor any arbitrary intervention into it.[9]

Thus for example it has been suggested that chaos theory can help our conception. This allows us to imagine God acting in energy and matter through an input of 'information', which affects outcomes but without manipulation. It involves, for Polkinghorne, the input of information at the quantum level in the initial conditions of any dynamic system – which then steers the process to produce different outcomes. For Peacocke, it involves God's input of information as an interaction at the macro-level, the world system as a whole, rather in the way that a human mind acts on the body as a whole. Both these are attempts to conceive a causal joint for divine action in a way which relates to natural causation rather than replaces it, yet without making the analogy between divine and natural causation so stretched that it ceases to have meaning. Both also extend the scope of this

---

[9] See, for example, John Polkinghorne, *Exploring Reality: The Intertwining of Science and Religion* (London: Yale University Press, 2005). Arthur Peacocke, *All That is: A Naturalistic Faith for the 21st Century* (Minneapolis: Fortress Press, 2007); *Theology for a Scientific Age* (London: SCM Press, 1993).

divine action in principle to the non-human world (i.e. God's action is not restricted just to the action of a transcendent mind on other minds).[10] This is also true of even more recent imagining of providence in scientific terms, in which providence is God's infusion of purposive presence specifically in the processes of evolution. Here, in the hands of Sarah Coakley, it is the co-operative tendencies of evolution which are seen as God's causal vehicle ultimately for bringing about acts of human altruism.[11] All these proposals allow for at least some sense that God is bringing about both general and specific outcomes through a kind of purposive action which is entirely integral with empirical processes.

Naturally there are limitations here too. Conceptually, the account of how information input can affect a specific outcome is still fragile. For Polkinghorne and others, it depends on a notion of 'collapsing' the wave function of probability so that it actualizes a particular outcome at a particular space or time, rather than merely carrying its possibility in its overall shape. This does not convince all.[12] There are also theological questions to be asked. God's action conceived in this way may still seem too constrained in principle by the structures of God's own created reality. This is a peril intrinsic to any natural theology where the meaning of God is related to what is recognizable in other empirical terms.[13] Nonetheless, the overall endeavour of this kind of approach remains suggestive – it certainly offers some new conceptual space in which theology can operate.

All these approaches therefore demonstrate a measure of new credibility in imagining divine causality. None may satisfy entirely, but at least they mark out some new conceptual possibilities. Moreover, they attempt to do this without entirely compromising the theological need to affirm the divine sovereignty,

---

[10] Cf. the account of divine action and natural order in Philip Clayton and Steven Knapp, *The Predicament of Belief* (Oxford: Oxford University Press, 2011), p. 59. Here the authors seem more unsure about this further scope of divine action within the 'non-mental' natural order. But they too do not rule it out. The mental realm is 'at least one sphere in which divine action can occur' (without overriding natural order).

[11] See Martin Nowak and Sarah Coakley (eds), *Evolution, Games, and God* (Cambridge, MA: Harvard University Press, 2013), ch. 20.

[12] See Nicholas Saunders, *Divine Action and Modern Science* (Cambridge: Cambridge University Press, 2002).

[13] For example, T. A. Smedes, *Chaos, Complexity and God: Divine Action and Scientism* (Dudley, MA: Peeters, 2004). For a more general survey of the potential and limits of this approach see also Christoph Lameter, *Divine Action in the Framework of Scientific Thinking: From Quantum Theory to Divine Action* (Newark: Christianity in the 21st Century, 2006). This literature is helpfully reviewed by Amos Yong, 'Divining "Divine Action" in Theology-Science', *Zygon*, 43 (2008), pp. 191–9.

freedom and transcendence. And in that sense they are all potentially constructive approaches, not reductive.

Combining approaches, new models

However, the real constructive advance comes, I suggest, whenever theology attempts to combine these sorts of different approaches. That is, when it offers unifying models which can capitalize on some of their best insights, without having to buy in to any one approach. Here we may be able to make even more progress.

So for example we could note Kevin Vanhoozer's recent attempt to do this.[14] He uses this multiplicity of approaches to propose a new *analogia auctori*; a picture of the God–world relationship where God is to the world as an author in creative relation to her work. Within that overall frame he can then conceive God making things happen by a model of causality which he describes as communicative action. This is a mode of 'making things happen' understood primarily as a relation of interactive communication which elicits a response; a model of the self as an effective agent through interdependence and responsiveness.

How might this work? In relation to the natural world, the model can operate mostly according to those insights of the scientist-theologians. That is, God's communicative action with the physical world is best understood as a kind of information that God inputs in the way that either Polkinghorne or Peacocke have envisaged. This is 'communication' only in a stretched sense, since the structures of non-sentient reality do not receive it or respond to it in a personally reciprocal way. Nonetheless it describes a way of acting in the world which is effective, while also respecting the integrity of the world and working within its grain, rather than interrupting it. So in that sense it is at least analogous to the way that the communication of speech and dialogue can work with persons.

In relation to humanity and human history, we can elaborate further. Drawing on Vanhoozer, but also going beyond him, it is easy to see how a basic analogy of communicative action can work in specific ways. First,

[14] Kevin Vanhoozer, *Remythologizing Theology: Divine Action, Passion, and Authorship* (Cambridge: Cambridge University Press, 2010).

we should see God's communicative action with humanity building on the account of the underlying divine causation in the natural order: that is, it occurs when the information put in to the natural or physical substructure of wider reality becomes part of human consciousness. This then gives us potential for recognition of God's act which releases an even greater potential for God to act through us. For when we are able to recognize this or that natural, historical, social or psychological event *as* a word of God (or at least as some sort of moral imperative) God has made his mind and will *known* – and this elicits an inevitable response of some kind.

This is not because God's communication has coerced our seeing and response, but because it is like a specific interjection in a dialogue. As such it will always have an effect and elicit a response, without overriding our freedom. We can see this in the way our own speech-acts have effect. When we communicate our mind and will we add information into the world which is never neutral. It has an effect. It changes the way other people act. To express our thoughts to someone else will cause a reaction in some way, however imperceptibly. Since even mere observation of another person or object apparently acts as an input of information to bring about some change at the quantum level, specific interjection will certainly do so.

Furthermore, the overall analogy of authorship also suggests how this kind of divine communicative action can be effective in a specifically sovereign way. As finite human agents our reach is limited; we cannot guarantee either that the response to our interjections will be as we wish, or that we can turn the response to our own ends. But in the case of the authorial God this is properly different. On the analogy of a transcendent author, God would have universal scope for this communicative action. In Vanhoozer's terms: 'the Author is omnitemporal, free to be present in and to all times'.[15]

In other words, God's 'interjections' are not just one other voice in a polyphonic world but a potentially omnipresent voice, of a different order. Divine interjections have this greater effect because they are not limited by finite access to us and to others around us. His interjections can both precede and follow all our reactions, shaping them at every point by new information. This means God is not reduced just to acting only passively or responsively to

---

[15] Vanhoozer, *Remythologizing Theology*, p. 323. He draws on both Barth and Bakhtin to make this point (cf. also p. 325).

his creatures. Instead, God has 'already' transformed the meaning of our actions into divine meaning because of the new context God can always provide for our own action.[16] With such universal scope of interjection divine sovereignty is therefore irresistible – in both particular and general outcomes – even though still operating co-operatively and not coercively.[17] As such, it is distinct from open theism and the 'kenotic-perichoretic' models of divine persuasion, which offer God only more limited causal effect.[18]

This re-framing of divine causality within the overall model of divine authorship combines insights from all the theological approaches previously outlined.[19] It draws on Barth's overall concern for faith and revelation to determine the shape of causality rather than vice versa, for it is pre-eminently the specific narratives of revelation which require this dramatic, dialogical and communicative understanding of the God–world relation.[20] Yet it also draws on natural theology and scientific notions of causality for its discourse of 'information input'. At the same time, it is built on an effort to press the analytical questions; that is, the attempt to show what effective personal divine action would actually mean, in relation to other discourse. Thus, for example, we can now refer to specific and differentiated divine action to mean the communication and realization of different kinds of *purposes* in different events, rather than empirical identification of a different kind of *causality* (which, being transcendent, is necessarily opaque).

To be sure, much will remain contestable. It is debatable whether the personalist language of divine action used within this model of communicative action genuinely translates as a form of causality, or simply as another logical form of explanation altogether. The extent to which it just stands alongside empirical and scientific discourse (as with Barth), or whether it transforms it, or in some other way integrates with it, remains moot. In other words, there are times when this sort of approach could still be seen as operating

---

[16] I previously elaborated a similar concept in White, *The Fall of a Sparrow*, chs 5 and 6.

[17] Vanhoozer, *Remythologizing Theology*, ch. 7. Here he is at pains to point out that the merely persuasive and not coercive nature of divine communicative action is nonetheless irresistible.

[18] Ibid., pp. 313–14.

[19] Ibid., p. xiii. Vanhoozer complains here that few theologians actually make use of all available resources.

[20] Barth himself actually claimed this relation must be conceived in 'communicative *rather* than causal' tems (though not in order to do away with the concept of causality altogether, just 'to avoid de-personalizing it'). See Vanhoozer, *Remythologizing Theology*, p. 28, cf. note 109. His indebtedness to Barth in his theological exposition of causality is explicit: see, for example, pp. 369ff.

with personalist language over against rational explanation, religious language over against scientific, rather than integrated with it – as if it is selling out to the Kantian dichotomy after all. Likewise its specific claim that God really can work irresistibly (i.e. sovereignly) through this personal non-mechanistic persuasive action is arguable.

Even so, the overall point surely remains. Given a wide mapping of theological approaches, corralled with the help of constructive analogies such as this, effective divine agency can still be constructively rethought in a variety of ways. There are new models for divine agency and divine causality, and there are significant conceptual and imaginative resources to support it. So we really do not need to lose our nerve about it.

Empirical issues: Imagining the basic shape of the story

But we must now turn to the more broadly empirical challenges as well. For even if we think divine agency is conceivable in principle, empirical challenges will still press in practice. It is a problem of identification. On what basis can we identify the presence and purposes of this agency? None of our conceptions of it allows us to look for this basis simply in the shape of ordinary causality itself – even though it may be operating *through* this causality. So how can it be identified at all? As noted at the outset, some events press this challenge to the utmost. How could divine agency for a good purpose ever be imagined, in any sense, in events which present themselves empirically just as downright evil? From Augustine to postmodernity we have seen this to be a critical issue. And so here too we need to explore further imaginings.

Foundations in Barth and Frei

In fact here again we do not start completely afresh. The previous mapping laid some foundations even if further work needs to be done. Not least, I suggest, those figural readings of Barth and Frei will offer a starting point. Together with some insights from Hodgson they can provide a useful basis, whatever their limitations. So again I will first recapitulate before suggesting how this might also then be further developed.

Thus first we should recall the key insistence from Barth and Frei on the pivotal hermeneutical role of the narrative of Christ (and more widely with Hodgson, the narratives of 'transforming praxis'). This is the claim that divine meaning can always be identified in specific events when they are brought into figural relation to that central Christ-shaped narrative of redemption, or when triangulated with other such transformative events.

It is significant because of its twofold implication. On the one hand it suggests that there *is* a way, in principle, of identifying the purpose of any particular event or sequence of events. A Christ-shaped meaning *is* there to be found – in all events. Barth, following Calvin, was certainly clear about this. God's activity can and does connect all events in this figural way to his christological purpose. On the other hand, in practice, it concedes that this meaning will often be hidden and deferred. That is inevitable when many of the connections are made in a 'secret' providence: that is, through a set of figural relationships with Christ beyond the reach of ordinary linear history. This figural pattern also means that the meaning we can nonetheless identify is unlikely to be visible in straightforward, long, linear narratives. It is more likely to be visible only in 'smaller' stories. In short: while God's purpose can in principle be identified anywhere, in practice we only tend to see it in fragments, scattered only sparsely throughout history.

For further clarification. On the one hand, this is clearly an account of purpose in events which assumes divine action really is *in* public history, not just beyond it. In other words, although much meaning may come from hidden relations beyond linear history, it does not dilute divine action merely to a spiritualized or allegorized meaning imposed on events. Barth and Frei are echoing Auerbach here: they offer a kind of figural reading which insists there is purposive divine action in historical narrative itself, not just in the spiritual ideas lying 'behind it' or allegorized by it. Put another way, it is a way of perceiving the meaning of divine action in the relationship between real events and persons, not just in underlying ideas or texts (as modernist and postmodernist constructions of meaning would have it). So in that sense this is certainly a full-blooded theology of history. On the other hand it is also clear that this account does not claim too much for history. For it also depends on that wider context of meaning in which these figural relations are made and a Christ-shaped purpose fulfilled. So this implies a transcendence of history for this action to be completed (of which more later), as well as an affirmation of history as the site of its reality.

In this way we have an account which resists a false dichotomy. It means that we are not bound to appeal either to an historical but wholly immanent source of meaning (impossible to square with some events), or to a transcendent but wholly a-historical source of meaning (impossible to square with Christology).[21] It suggests a providence radically and universally rooted in history, yet which also relies properly on its transcendence as well. It offers a real (i.e. historical) criterion of discernment in Christ, yet is also acutely aware that this meaning can only be seen in other events figurally, not read off easily from the actual linear shapes of history.

As such, this is indeed a promising foundation for credible belief. Yet of course it is still only a bare outline. It remains largely as picture of providence in principle, not in practice. So in that sense the empirical questions still press, especially the questions of identification. Apart from the Christ event itself, what other events can be identified as particularly load-bearing for discerning the meaning of things? Can we at least say more about what *sort* of events might count in this way? Above all can we say something more about those events which seem utterly opposed to divine purpose? The assertion that there are always hidden or 'transcendent' figural connections to give meaning to these events may be a necessary answer, but it will not be sufficient. It may seem empty, or worse, if we cannot say anything more. If will seem enclosed in its own fideism. It would certainly make any attempt at a public theology virtually impossible. So – can we go still further?

Providence and public theology: Using Frei and Hodgson to go beyond Barth

When we press these questions on Barth himself we find he does take us just a little further, especially in the matter of identification. He cites, for example, the history of the Jews, the Bible and the church. These at least can be definitely identified as providential signs of God's specific purposes of divine revelation.[22]

---

[21] As John Dawson has pointed out, this dichotomy was also rejected in pre-critical figural readings: Dawson, *Christian Figural Reading and the Fashioning of Identity.*

[22] Barth, *CD* III/3, pp. 200ff.

He points also to the events of particular scriptural narratives to yield reliable meaning and witness – if subject to a process of exegesis.

This is clearest when Barth is expounding God's specific purposes of election.[23] Thus in his doctrine of election he offers detailed exegesis of a whole range of disparate Old Testament narratives – its patriarchial narratives, levitical ceremonial and history of kingship – all of which connect through Christ in order to bear witness to divine purpose about election. In true figural fashion they are not immediately causally connected to each other, nor do they simply repeat each other, for they each have their own unique historical integrity and must not be flattened into mere ciphers for 'eternal truths'; yet by this figural reference to each other through a wider context of meaning in Christ they nonetheless yield common true divine purpose within them.

If the emphasis is switched from election to liberation we could also then use the story of Passover and Exodus in a similar way, bringing them alongside Christ event to yield specific meaning. Barth does not do this as clearly here as he does with election, but the same principle can apply. The stories are separated by centuries, their history is contested, their historical connections unclear, and they have different human actors and actions attributed to them (some unsavoury). Yet we still see the family resemblance, the common identity of one common underlying actor. Liberation is the common purpose. Both cry out 'God's hand is at work in this, the same God, – a *liberating* God!' – not because we can trace this God in all the intervening events between Moses and Jesus to join their story in visible ways, but precisely as a figural connection; there is a scent of the same sort of person as the beating heart of them both.

However, Barth cannot really take us much beyond this specific sacred history. When pushed to name particular events or narratives in wider 'secular' history he is less helpful. Although he affirms the fact of God's purposes everywhere, particular secular events only yield, for him, faint signs and traces of this – even with figural readings.[24] This means, for example, that he was reluctant explicitly to endorse even such positive movements as the spread of democracy or the formation of the United Nations as God's specific providential action. This was interpreted by his critics as political indifference,

---

[23] Arguably, is in the doctrine of election more than any other that Barth comes closest to specifying the actual meaning of providence in any world occurrence cf. Kennedy, *Providence and Personalism*, ch. 6.

[24] Barth, *CD* III/3, pp. 196–9.

a failure in his public theology. Barth vigorously denied this: arguably, both his life and theology as a whole was in fact profoundly connected with actual social and political realities of his time.[25] But it remains the case that he was unwilling to make these sorts of definitive judgements in the secular realm. It is all of a piece both with his rejection of natural theology and his wish to treat secular history with its own integrity (i.e. not to impose theological meaning on it reductively or arbitrarily). Understandable, but undoubtedly restricting.

Yet although Barth is limiting here, could we draw more from Frei? Admittedly, he too was wary of making absolute specific judgements about secular affairs. He conceded they had their own historical integrity and narrative logic. So he too accepted that the figural meaning of events in God's purposes will usually be 'another' meaning, often opaque (deriving, in Frei's terms, from Christ who is a unique 'unsubstitutable' reality). But it is also clear that Frei was not content to leave it there. He wanted something more of a *public* theology of providence which could be identified more widely in secular events.[26] What Frei was prepared to look for, therefore, when triangulating events with Christ, was at least a relative judgement even if not an absolute one – which could then free a wider canvas for identifying meaning in more kinds of events.

Put another way, Frei used figural readings to identify some secular sub-narratives as at least having a more direct relation to divine purpose than others. As such, although their ultimate place in an (invisible) overall pattern of purpose is still unknowable, a proximate judgement can still sometimes be made. For example Frei cites politically liberal 'progressive' polices in contrast to 'revolution': theology can at least endorse policies of the former more than the latter, even if it withholds absolute judgement about them. This in no way implies reverting to a doctrine of linear progress. It is not the claim that these policies will bring in the kingdom of God in any straight line. But it is a claim that they can at least be seen as events which fall more decisively within the overall shape of the kingdom than others.[27]

---

[25] See Tim Gorringe, *Karl Barth: Against Hegemony* (Oxford: Oxford University Press, 1999).

[26] This is Higton's overall thesis in *Christ, Providence and History*.

[27] Cf. Higton, *Christ, Providence and History*, p. 170: he ascribes Frei's cautious advance into a more public theology to the influence of H. Richard Niebuhr. Cf. Frei's paper, 'H. Richard Niebuhr on History, Church Nation' (1988).

We could press this approach still further if we use other secular (non-biblical) events as examples. For instance, we could consider Constantine's conversion and Constantinianism in similar light. Like almost all events it has ambiguity. If triangulated with the diaspora as a normative model for church (i.e. as a pilgrim people) then it can be represented as the 'Fall of the Church', a damaging compromise of Christian mission by collusion with secular power from which we are still needing to be rescued. Alternatively, if triangulated with a normative model of Davidic monarchy, it can be represented as a fulfilment for the church leading eventually to the saving spread of Christian values in the world. Both have been proposed, even though they are diametrically opposed – and this can lead to cynicism about all providential interpretation. Yet it need not if we are willing to look through this lens of a greater or lesser 'degree' of figural providential meaning. That is, it can be identified as having a more decisive part to play in God's overall purposes than some other events, yet without requiring us to interpret it either as outright judgement or vindication, nor even as *uniquely* significant in any respect. Instead it can be seen simply as one particularly significant but unfinished part of what William Cavanaugh describes as 'the long pedagogy of God's people': that is, a particular focus of meaning which contains both judgement and vindication, still not fully resolved.[28]

In other words, here is a principle that allows us to make a judgement about a particular event which accepts that its ultimate meaning is still being determined (so it must not itself become determinative of all other narratives), yet which also allows us to affirm that the event does have particular divine meaning – and more so than some other more routine events in the world.

We could draw on Hodgson too to endorse this sort of approach. If we extend the principle, as we must, beyond narrow ecclesial, Christian, euro-centric concerns, then *any* event which embodies some christological 'shape of freedom' could be identified in this way: that is, as a more direct part of God's purposes of pedagogy than some others, but without needing to claim a definitive meaning for it. This could be extended to other events with the shape of other christological meanings, not just those with the shape of

---

[28] Cf. William Cavanaugh, 'What Constantine Has to Teach Us', in John Roth (ed.), *Constantine Revisited: Leithart, Yoder and the Constantinian Debate* (Eugene, OR: Wipf & Stock, 2013), pp. 83–99.

liberation. Any event which embodies reconciliation, covenant, or redemption, could count in the same degree.

Quash might also agree, if we appropriated his methodology in a similar way. As noted, much of his 'found' theology is dealing only with the epistemological questions involved (i.e. how our attention is drawn to their significance by a process of reception, or by some element of surprise which provokes a process of abductive reasoning from that event to a more general meaning).[29] Yet in fact what underlies the concern with how our attention is drawn is a straightforward substantive supposition; namely, as a matter of fact, some events do have a more intense significance than others (without denying some significance to all other events as well).

In such ways, therefore, figural readings can deal credibly with identifiable events. It is an approach which can identify some special status in at least some particular events, in so-called secular history as well as sacred. In other words, there is some substantive empirical credibility here, not just a formal but empty system of belief. Equally, just because a figural interpretation does not ride roughshod over the realities of history, it can also remain cautious, reticent and relative in its judgements, rather than imposing absolute meanings – and this too lends credibility. Especially in relation to the more surd and evil events of life.

The approach also remains theologically credible. That is to say, to achieve this empirical credibility a figural approach does not have to trim its theological sails by reducing in principle the full scope of divine action and the assumption of radical sovereignty and transcendence which underlies that principle. It can remain committed to a universal providence, even where it is opaque, precisely because even specific judgements are only relative. In this way it does justice to the full theological tradition behind providence, as well as to the full range of empirical challenges it faces in late modernity.

To be sure, public theology may still want more than this, and prophetic discernment about particular events will certainly want to be more specific and decisive in some of its judgements. Yet a credible doctrine of providence has a different task to either public theology or prophecy. Its function is to articulate the overall belief that God is at work in events, not necessarily to make final

---

[29] Cf. Quash, *Found Theology*, pp. 156–7, 215–16.

judgements about all specific occasions. And in those terms perhaps this sort of overall picture we have re-imagined here *is* sufficient.

Imagining transcendence

Yet there is also one other final challenge. Can we also imagine an adequate concept of transcendence to undergird all this? The requirement to do so has been implicit throughout, Some notion of transcendence has been assumed simply for the credibility any concept of divine agency within history at all. But it also becomes necessary with this appeal to the hidden figural meanings of that action, forced on us in the face the baffling nature of so many actual events.[30] Because the fulfilment of those meanings could only lie 'behind' history, a concept of transcendence is vital here too. Their hidden redemptive meanings will depend on some transcendent transaction. Specifically, they will depend on a wholly different kind of time and place where connections to an eternal Christ can be forged by God. Without this, some events would be left ultimately random after all. And although that might not matter much for routine happenstances of life, it surely matters for the major goods and evils of life. If these too are purely random it would call into question the providence of a good God right at its roots.

So it is clearly important to secure this assumption of transcendence. It matters to be able to think of a realm of reality beyond our current empirical experience where *any* event can find some redemptive meaning. But can we? This is the challenge.[31]

A challenge not always taken up

It is important to pursue this because although some general notion of transcendence is implied by most theologians in most contexts, the challenge

---

[30] This need to stipulate transcendence was also trailed in our previous analysis of narrative. If a full range of non-linear figural meanings are to have substance, then the form of narrative to which they belong must transcend what is provided just by human mind or human agency. See above, Chapter 1, pp. 26–9.

[31] In particular, the challenge is to show how such events could be brought into relation with some *intrinsically* good redemptive meaning. Finding an intrinsically good meaning and purpose is necessary for redemption. That is to say, meaning cannot be simply instrumental to some other good. That would not satisfy a good purpose for human subjects. If we are ends in God's purpose,

to imagine it specifically in relation to universal redemption has not always explicitly been taken up.[32] Barth and Frei are particularly tantalizing here. They assume (and require) much which is not specifically expounded.

Thus Barth certainly affirms transcendence generally. It is essential to his theology. It denotes God's ontological otherness, and especially God's absolute freedom (the freedom to be immanent, passible, 'weak', as well as eternal, impassible, sovereign).[33] Yet he does not then specifically explore how this relates to the redemption of all things through Christ: that is, he does not specify what sort of transcendent realm of being and action must be implied for Christ's universal redemptive purpose to actually take effect (in history or eternity).

This is evident when he is expounding his doctrine of election. As we saw, Barth affirmed a fulfilment of election by displaying typological connections of some events with Christ. But this is done largely by exegesis of texts, not by any exposition of how a transcendent Christ might reach across time and space to make such election real for them. Likewise with the doctrine of providence. He affirms that all 'worldly occurrences' will also be connected with Christ's redemptive purpose (implying some transcendent realm to make such connection), but does not venture any more to support it. He asserts there will be a 'final manifestation' of this overruling of all things in Jesus Christ, but says no more about how this is secured. He claims that 'one day' in the eschatological moment we will be able to see how God in Christ is Lord both of the general and the particular; but until then God only 'laughs' at any attempt to see His rule, and so there is reluctance to say more what this entails.[34]

This is even more apparent in Frei. He does not deny some general transcendent reference to theology. But he does not develop its meaning.

---

not just means, only a meaning which relates *internally* to our own good will count in what befalls us. This sharpens the challenge even further. See further below, pp. 134, 150.

[32] In fact even a general notion of transcendence is not always assumed. Oliver Davies, for example, is wary of all talk of transcendence. It implies for him an unacceptable metaphysical dualism. Moreover, anything 'beyond' space and time can only be pointed to from within space and space and time, which leaves the concept of transcendence itself vacuous – all we have is the act of pointing. Cf. Oliver Davies, Paul Janz and Clemens Sedmark, *Transformation Theology* (London: T & T Clark, 2007), pp. 42, 43 .This sounds a proper cautionary note, but in my view it certainly should not deter all talk of transcendence. Radical transcendence is not dualistic precisely because it is radical: that is, it overcomes distinctions rather than enforcing them. The trajectory of pointing is relevant to this radical transcendence because it can intimate land beyond horizons, even though itself firmly embedded this side of those horizons. On this issue see further below, pp. 129, 134.

[33] Barth, *CD* IV/1 (Edinburgh: T & T Clark, 1961), pp. 186–8.

[34] Barth, *CD* III/3, pp. 41, 242ff.

In fact he is particularly wary of this. I detect this reticence in a number of ways. It arises first out of his positive concern to do justice to 'realistic' (i.e. history-like and public) readings of scripture, and to distinguish this from the 'repeatable' or 'mythic', which he rejects. Myth, for Frei, has to do with a 'not directly representable psychic or cosmic state' which 'transcends finite particular occurrences' – and so it is discredited along with all idealist-romantic philosophy which fails to grasp the public reality of history-like narrative.[35] The trouble is, this means the actual idea of transcendence has appeared only in relation to something he is rejecting.

Wariness about transcendence also arises from Frei's related concern to assert the 'identity' of Jesus Christ in events of history, as distinct from his presence. The presence of Christ would imply something repeatable, which detracts from the unique and unsubstitutable character of the Christ event. Meaning for Frei, therefore, is not derived by Christ repeating his presence in our lives and our histories, as if from some transcendent source of timeless presence. Instead, it supervenes by mirroring in our life the specific 'shape' or 'identity' of his life and history.[36] This preserves the integrity of history. But again, it has the consequence of relegating the discourse of transcendence to something he is rejecting.

Frei's positive concern to affirm the identity of Christ in concrete ways illustrates this in yet another way. Identity generally for Frei is given in, rather than hidden by, public events and actions in history-like narrative. This is in line with Gilbert Ryle, for whom there is no transcendent ghost in the machine lying behind our historical actions and interactions but only an embodied unity of intention-in-action.[37] Here again notions of transcendence have occurred in what is discredited – and no positive alternative imaginings of transcendence are developed in their place. So when it comes to Frei's figural readings of history and God's agency it is not surprising that there is little explicit reference to a transcendence here either. There is no specific exploration of that transcendent 'place' or perspective in which this agency operates to give meaning. It is part and parcel of Frei's general reticence to address the nature of transcendence in any formulation of meaning.

---

[35] See Hans Frei, 'Theological Reflections on the Accounts of Jesus' Death and Resurrection', *Christian Scholar* 49 (1966), pp. 263–306; cf. also Frei, *The Eclipse of Biblical Narrative*, pp. 242–4.

[36] Cf. Hans Frei, 'A Meditation for the Week of Good Friday and Easter' (1974), printed in Frei, *The Identity of Jesus Christ*, pp. 168–73: cf. Higton, *Christ, Providence and History*, p. 109.

[37] Frei, *The Identity of Jesus Christ*, p. 92.

Why does this happen? For Frei himself, we may speculate. Perhaps, as Higton has pointed out, it is because Frei thought of himself more as a historian than a theologian. As such, perhaps he thought that credibility in his context required a concentration on the historical and reticence about the transcendent. Whereas for Barth, I suspect the reticence about articulating transcendence was less to do with establishing credibility, and much more to do ensuring his theology of revelation did not get subsumed within a wider metaphysic.

But whatever the reason, we can hardly rest content with this. As we have seen, if we are imagining providence, a notion of transcendence is too important a foundation to be sidelined. A doctrine of providence without that support would be left dangerously lopsided. So here we again need to go further than such as Barth and Frei. To sustain a credible providence we need to give some more meaning to transcendence. It must itself be mappable in some way, not just left implicit. If not, it will simply be dismissed just as a cipher for mystery – and providence will be dismissed with it.

Attempts to meet the challenge: Some meanings of transcendence

In fact the notion of transcendence has not had to stand in theology entirely without some supporting conceptual analysis – in spite of obvious difficulties in articulating it. There have been several ways of gesturing to it and exploring it. Broadly speaking, it has received two meanings in recent theological use (there are anachronistic elements in using the word in English at all before the nineteenth century). These can be set out simply as follows.

To begin with, when the word has been applied to the early tradition of classical theism, it has come to denote a very radical otherness in the being of God. This sets strict limits to what can be known clearly about God and what can be said about God. In this account, especially applied to Aquinas, God's being is radically different from all other beings because God alone has necessary rather than derived being: God is not the greatest being, nor even the sum of all being, but the unique ground of all being. As such, God is not ultimately comparable with the rest of reality in his being. God is to the world more like a dreamer to a dream or an author to a book, than a parent to a child or a whole to a part. It follows that we can only speak of God through analogy in which a radical unlikeness is just as important as any supposed similarity.[38] In short, whatever possibilities faith and revelation may provide for knowing God and relating to him, God's transcendence must always qualify them. God's absolute otherness remains the ultimate limit and frame for knowledge of God. God, by definition, is another order of being altogether. This radical transcendence does not render God's order of being entirely nonsensical to us as some have suggested.[39] That is because language derived from our order of being can, by analogy, at least *point* to that which is beyond itself, much as a sign in one landscape can point to another over a horizon while itself remaining wholly embedded on its own side.[40] Nonetheless, as such, radical transcendence does indeed refer to that which is wholly *sui generis*.

This first 'strong' meaning of transcendence can also be applied more widely in Western philosophy and religion. Calvin Schrag, for example, tracks it back through mystical traditions in the 'ineffable One of Plotinus', Eckhart's 'Godhead', through to Rudolf Otto's 'Idea of the Holy', Kiekegaard's appeal to paradox, and the 'All-Encompassing' of Karl Jaspers' existential philosophy. Moving into late modernity, he also sees a similar conceptual structure lying behind the ethical intentions of Levinas. In order to define our fundamental ethical obligation as absolute and asymmetrical, rather than relative and reciprocal, Levinas marked out a locus of transcendent otherness which is 'outside' all shared categories of being.[41] As we saw earlier with Simon Critchley, this extends the meaning of transcendence beyond the metaphysics of theism – yet it is still an exploration of the same kind of meaning of radical transcendence which theism has itself employed.

The second meaning, however, is less radical. This derives from applying it to Scotus and others in later medieval theology who talked more freely of God and creatures 'sharing' the property of 'being', even if not in the same way. This opened the door to the claim that we can know and speak of God more directly. It has led to a notion of divine transcendence in which there is at least some comparison possible with creaturely reality, even if just by

---

[38] Arguably Aquinas did not have any real theory of analogy to help negotiate this difference: but that itself is indication of how radical it is conceived to be. Cf. David Burrell, *Aquinas, God and Action* (Notre Dame, IN: University of Notre Dame Press, 1979), p. 55.

[39] For example, John Caputo in Orrin Summerell (ed.), *The Otherness of God* (Charlottesville: University of Virginia Press, 1998).

[40] See above p. 126, note 32; see also p. 134.

[41] See Calvin Schrag, *The Self after Postmodernity* (New Haven: Yale University Press, 1997), ch. 4.

contrast. So since the nineteenth century the term 'transcendence' has been used mostly in contrast to the notion of immanence (i.e. God is 'beyond', 'distant' 'unengaged', rather than 'near', 'close' and 'engaged'). As such, God's transcendence asserts difference but it is still a difference in the same register of reality: it must be in the same overall order of being because it draws meaning in relation to that order, if only a relation of contrast and difference. It is no longer a way of defining a reality in which all our normal human categories simply break down altogether.[42]

Transcendence and universal divine agency in history

These two outline meanings of transcendence are simplified. But at least they show there is some sort of conceptual hinterland to choose from. And even without further refinement this helps clarify the meaning required here.

For a start, it clearly signals the kind of meaning of transcendence needed to support any basic (credible) divine agency in history. *Prima facie* the second might seem more attractive. A God who is not radically other appears more accessible. But in fact that is exactly what makes a notion of divine agency incredible, because any agency which is *not* radically other in relation to creaturely causality will displace or compete with it. This makes it empirically problematic, at odds with science. It is also theologically problematic, compromising either creaturely autonomy or divine sovereignty.

By contrast, the first and more radical notion of transcendence bypasses these problems and clearly makes divine agency more credible. It opens up conceptual space for an agency which does not compete at all in the same order of being. The notion of a wholly different kind of divine being and action means there is no need and no sense in asking 'where' God is or acts in comparison with or contrast to other beings or causes within the world. As such, this kind of action can then 'join' or 'incorporate' all these others with integrity: that is, without competing with them or displacing them.

In short, the more radical view of transcendence, far from distancing or excluding God's action from the world, is actually the ground of it – as we

---

[42] Cf. Placher, *The Domestication of Transcendence*, pp. 6, 7. Placher traces this process of reduced or 'domesticated' transcendence from the seventeenth century onwards. He draws on Kathryn Tanner's discussion of transcendence in *God and Creation in Christian Theology: Tyranny or Empowerment* (Oxford: Blackwell, 1988).

saw earlier with Barth.[43] It is how we can say God is everywhere, relates to everything and causes everything – not instead of other agents but in and through them.[44] As such, radical transcendence permits a truly universal scope of action. The most fitting analogy to convey this, as we saw with Vanhoozer, is that of the author or playwright and her work. Because the author exists as a different order of being and reality she is not limited to acting alongside or instead of her characters in the occasional voice of a narrator, but can act through *all* her characters, in the *whole* plot and in *every* action.

Transcendence of time and divine redemption beyond history

This more radical view of transcendence also best supports credible divine agency beyond history – to provide these necessary hidden meanings which providence requires. In particular, it entails for God's agency the kind of radical transcendence of *time* which is necessary for this sort of universal redemption. Only a radical transcendence of time can provide the possibility of new redemptive meanings being forged by divine action in a dimension which 'ordinary' history alone has clearly not provided.[45]

This specific transcendence of time is integral to the broader claim of radical transcendence that God is not a causally or temporally derived being but the eternal ground of all being. It also follows from the essential meaning of any perfect agency in itself. All personal action seeks meaning, a meaning which often lies in more than one present moment of time: that is, it requires some wider context of past and future events to complete that meaning.[46] It is

---

[43] See pp. 97, 111–12 above.

[44] William Placher presses home these implications very clearly. Thus: 'If we ask Aquinas or Luther or Calvin, Where is God? Or, concerning the tornado, the rain that broke the drought, the airplane crash or our neighbor's act of kindness, Who did it? God or some other agent? they refuse to answer to answer the question posed in those terms. ... They say, with only limited qualifications, that God causes all these events. Their accounts do not even permit us to say that God and some other agents collaborated in bringing about events, assigning a percentage of responsibility to each. Yes, they say, X was the result of human decision, or natural force, or accident – but also, X was fully the result of God's will' (Placher, *The Domestication of Transcendence*, p. 112). As theodicy this can sound brutally uncompromising. Yet simply as an explication of how radical transcendence helps convey a distinctively divine form of 'action' in all kinds of events it makes the point well. Such radical transcendence permits universal scope of action.

[45] Even Quash, who is rightly concerned throughout that meaning is not be found simply in an escape from time, requires for the fulfilment of his figural meanings a kind of transcendent context – for it is a context in which 'all times are present to one another in God' (Quash, *Found Theology*, p. 112).

[46] Cf. Quash, *Found Theology*, p. 218. There needs to be a sphere (referred through signs) in which 'it is possible responsibly to relate to the objects one encounters as more than discrete and atomistic units'.

a familiar point: an 'atomized' action (e.g. picking up a stick) always requires a wider sub-narrative to determine its meaning (e.g. playing with a dog, building a log cabin, hitting an enemy).[47] So, as such, no perfect purposive action could ever be wholly and solely 'present' – it must already include some memory of the immediate past and anticipation of the future to give it meaning: that is, it requires a wider trans-temporal context.[48]

The analogy of the author is again pertinent. God's vantage point needs to be very like that of an author in creating her work, who traverses the whole time sequence of her work in the creation of it. That is what helps determine the meaning in any one part of it. The analogy fails to the extent that the order of independent reality with which God works when God is creating this world is more radically other than, and greater than, that of a fictional world. But in fact even when human writers deal with fictional worlds they often talk of working with a sense of radical 'otherness' in their characters, some intimation that they have 'a life of their own'.[49] In that sense the analogy holds quite well.

God construed in this way, as radically transcendent ground of all being who acts from beyond time as well as within it, is therefore the clear basis we need. God is in a position always to re-frame temporal events to give them new (redemptive) meaning. It is a construal which means we are conceiving a dimension in which events in history can always be brought into new relations with other events (historical and eternal) to give them such meaning. In particular, it means that all events could be redeemed by being brought into a new relation specifically with the event of Christ (which is itself conceived as an eternal as well as historical event, and can therefore be recapitulated in all other events – this transcendent status of the Christ event being of course one of most distinctive soteriological claims of the tradition).[50]

---

[47] This in no way implies that the meaning of divine action in particular events is merely general or uniform (any more than playing, building or hitting are the same): it is simply to point out that these differentiated meanings of divine action in all particular events actually require a wider context than the particular temporal location of that event in itself.

[48] This recalls the notion of the extended specious present. Cf. my discussion in White, *The Fall of a Sparrow*, pp. 148ff.

[49] For example, Dorothy Sayer's celebrated discussion of this in *The Mind of The Maker* (London: Victor Gollancz, 1941). Others disagree, of course: notably J.-P. Sartre in *What is Literature?* He claimed the human author meets nothing but his own subjectivity. But George Steiner would have supported Sayers: he argues strongly that the creative artist is responding not just creating out of the self, but also responding to something beyond the self. See George Steiner, *Real Presences* (Chicago: University of Chicago Press, 1989).

[50] The belief that 'the lamb slain before the foundation of the world' constitutes the redemption of the whole world was developed in patristic theology from foundational New Testament images. I argued

Defending transcendence?

To be sure, this appeal to radical transcendence also begs questions. I have already responded to the most basic and general objection.[51] But there are others it must deal with too. These are conceptual, theological and moral – as follows.

The conceptual difficulties often begin in the attempt to combine any sort of notion of eternity with any sort of personal action. This is particularly the case if God's transcendence of time is taken to require God to be wholly timeless in God's own self. Personal action, after all, requires some sort of temporal reference to have any meaning at all, which a timeless God would negate. There is also an unresolved issue about the kind of divine omniscience which this universal scope of action would require. For if the scope of meaningful divine action is fully to include the future (including future free acts of creatures), without determinism, it implies God has a capacity for foreknowledge which includes 'middle knowledge': that is, the knowledge of what might have been with different creaturely input as well as what 'will' be as each input of information or creaturely action ensues – and such middle knowledge has received short shrift from a number of commentators.[52]

Yet there are responses to these conceptual difficulties. The fear that divine eternity must preclude divine all sense of personhood and temporality only presents itself on the basis of a contrastive notion of transcendence. Yet a radical transcendence bypasses the issue because it is not defined simply by contrast with time. As such, it still allows God's eternity to incorporate God's own kind of time.[53] As for middle knowledge, it is hard to see how any decisive argument could ever settle this either way. The arguments are speculative on either side, heavily dependent on unverifiable metaphysics and all arguable.[54] So these conceptual (and metaphysical) difficulties are hardly decisive.

---

and expounded in more detail this constitutive nature of the eternal Christ's redemptive act in Vernon White, *Atonement and Incarnation* (Cambridge: Cambridge University Press, 1991).

[51] That is, Caputo's claim that, strictly speaking, it cannot refer to anything with any sense at all. See above p. 129.

[52] For example, William Hasker, *God, Time and Knowledge* (Ithaca: Cornell University Press, 1989). Brian Hebblethwaite echoes this specifically in relation to the doctrine of providence in *Philosophical Theology and Christian Doctrine*, see especially ch. 8.8:4.

[53] See my earlier discussion of time and eternity in White, *Fall of a Sparrow*: other discussions have also seen possibilities of combining the two.

[54] Thus, for example, Thomas Flint finds it possible to mount a defence of some kind of Middle Knowledge, even if others cannot. Cf. Thomas Flint, 'Providence and Predestination', in Philip Quinn and Charles Taliaferro (eds), *A Companion to Philosophy of Religion* (Oxford: Blackwell, 1997), pp. 569–76.

The theological and historical objections usually centre on the old canard that it is always bound to short-change history. Any appeal to a redemptive meaning beyond history tends to provoke this sort of distrust. 'Transcendence' may seem to resonate too much with pre-modern pictures which deny the significance of history and narrative, or later tendencies which dilute them to idealism, ignoring that overwhelming turn to history we charted and the centrality of temporality and history in incarnational theology.

Yet here too there are responses. As already argued, the nature of narrative itself suggests that although 'ordinary' historical narrative may well be a necessary site of meaning, it is not sufficient.[55] In any case, this transcendence is certainly not a turn away from history, time and narrative altogether. As ground of all being it is in fact a radical affirmation of both eternity *and* time. As such, this picture of transcendent redemption is not simply the creation of another world of events; it is precisely the temporal world of events being redeemed in this transcendental way. More specifically, such ultimate redemption clearly still depends on history, as well as eternity, in the event of Christ itself. For it is always the Christ of history who is a pivot within that final alchemy in eternity. It is also the Christ of history who displays in history the full shape of what lies for some events only finally in eternity: that is, a shape of cross, resurrection and ascension; a transformation of pain and evil into a good which is complete because it is not only external (for others) but also internal (for the subject). For all these reasons this appeal to radical transcendence is certainly no mere idealism. It is grounded in empirical realities, not on a purely abstract idea of redemption.

Lastly, the moral objections arise if this appeal to transcendence attempts to 'explain' final redemption. For any claim to explain or transform meaning by reference to something else beyond itself raises the spectre of instrumentalism. Does it mean that evil has been 'used' for greater good? And does that in turn mean it has been *intended* for it? Has evil therefore been justified in some way? If so, this notion of universal redemption, far from being a theological necessity, might also seem a theological horror. Better, it may be thought, to leave God as a vulnerable fellow-sufferer of evil, and some evil unredeemed, rather than to imagine this kind of final but tainted triumph over it.

---

[55] See above pp. 26–9.

But here again there is a response. In broad terms we still need to ask: which is more tolerable – a transcendent and sovereign creator who can and does ultimately redeem all, or a vulnerable God whose creative endeavour always carried the risk that God would only be able to suffer and weep with us? I shall argue later it must be the former. I shall also qualify – and clarify – exactly what is meant by this final process of redemption: that is, I will make clear that what God is 'using' in this picture of transcendental redemption is not evil per se. As such, the moral challenge is certainly mitigated, if not refuted.[56]

So I believe this sort of appeal to radical transcendence remains possible and defensible, as well as vital. And as such it should not be short-changed, or left implicit, just out of embarrassment. As we saw earlier, talk of transcendence is too easily relegated to pre-modernity or left implicit for fear of losing empirical credibility – yet in fact theology is actually *less* credible without it, precisely because it undergirds so much central Christian doctrine of redemption, including providence. This is why transcendence must be named as well as assumed, and must not be allowed to slip out of view by default.[57]

Transcendence, eschatology and history: Pressing the case with Paul Fletcher

Finally, to cement this last point, I will refer to an essay by the late Paul Fletcher which resonates with much of what I have been arguing.[58] For he too believed theology has retreated from a fully transcendent cosmology, but should not. He also warned against taking history too readily as the sole source of meaning

---

[56] See pp. 149–53.

[57] In fact transcendence is still often left only implicit, in spite of some new theological interest in it (e.g. in mystical theology, or in Placher's discussion already cited). Or else it is treated only to critique its more inadequate metaphors. Thus Tillich and the radical theologies of the 1960s rightly offered critiques of traditional spatial metaphors for God's transcendence (God relating to us from 'above') because they fail to convey the divine uniqueness. However, their preferred metaphors of depth (God as 'ground of being'), like Moltmann and Pannenberg's temporal metaphors (God relating to us from 'the future'), still do not fully convey a radical transcendence. Likewise, process and narrative theologies, which have stressed the relational, open and immanent nature of God's activity within history have not denied transcendence, yet they have not usually conveyed it explicitly – they have tended to displace it beyond the remit of relevant discussion. The same can be said of most postmodern theologies. For a survey of the role of transcendence in 20th century Western theology see, for example, Stanley Grenz and Roger Olsen, *twentieth Century Theology: God and the World in a Transitional Age* (Carlisle: Paternoster Press, 1992).

[58] Paul Fletcher, *Disciplining the Divine: Towards an (Im)political Theology* (Farnham: Ashgate, 2009). Although an idiosyncratic (and unfinished) work, it is highly suggestive.

just for the sake of historical and empirical relevance and credibility. So he too wanted to reinvigorate a notion of transcendence. His discussion is broader, dealing with transcendence in a wider systematic frame (he discusses this primarily in the context of the doctrine of the Trinity). But the underlying issues remain the same.

Thus Fletcher first describes an overemphasis on immanence and neglect of radical transcendence specifically in the idea of a social Trinity. There he considers this has had the effect of evacuating any conceptual or metaphysical distance between God and human persons, conceiving them too closely to each other.[59] He then presses this question even harder in relation to the doctrine's claims to social, political and cultural relevance. One of the claims of the social Trinity is that it leads to better social and political modelling; that is, the perichoretic picture of indwelling and mutually constitutive persons of God, in contrast to monarchical or hierarchical pictures, is said to model a less oppressive and more relational way of being. Fletcher has no objection to this in itself. But he objects to a process it displays in which historical order and divine meaning, politics and religion, have effectively become identified with each other.

Fletcher traces this in part (as we have seen earlier) to Spinoza's monism in which there is no separation between divine and worldly reality, and to Hegel whose process of dialectic absorbs all time into the process and leaves no space for transcendence. Thus 'a temporality that was once reliant on creation, providence, and an integral relation to another time and space of consummation [that is, eschatology], has now itself become Absolute *in history*'.[60] The trouble is, this leaves insufficient transcendence in Christian eschatology to challenge the state's power when it appeals to history for its authority. For when the processes of history have become the sole resource for ultimate meaning, how can they be questioned?

Fletcher then follows through this trajectory specifically in a critique of Moltmann. Moltmann condemns the sort of monotheism which translates into political autocracy, and which legitimates particular political realities on the basis that they perform the divine will without remainder. Again, Fletcher would have no objection to this in itself. But he still sees Moltmann himself falling into

---

[59] That is, as just 'rational symbols of communicative action'.
[60] Fletcher, *Disciplining the Divine*, p. 120 (emphasis mine).

the same sort of trap. For Moltmann's own theology (i.e. the social model) would also too readily and absolutely legitimate a political arrangement. It might be a preferable politics but it has still become too absolutized. This is because he has a 'generalised judgement about the integrity of this concept'.[61] In other words, any process with an any sort of idealist (theological) construction of the 'right' sort of political community repeats the mistaken Hegelian move of identifying a religious ideal and a perfect state too easily, without allowing the critique of a transcendental eschatology. In Fletcher's view, Moltmann has succumbed to this because he has idealized liberal politics which sees this life and its survival to be ultimate, a *telos* which must be realized immanently. The intention may be honourable, but the outcome is a theology which has no resources to see how impoverished any purely immanent 'end' must be. Ultimately, it fails to move us beyond self-interest.[62]

Fletcher's cultural critique of the social Trinity raises a similar issue, again showing the impoverishing effect of giving priority to immanence In order to address the crisis of cultural relevance (in which atheism thrives by debunking mystery) theology has felt it could only address contemporary culture by '*refusing* the mystery' of divine transcendence. A largely univocal analogy between human relations and divine reality is the outcome.[63] The consequence is, again, to be in thrall to relevance and the spirit of the age, in particular its immanentism. This in turn means it has no resources to critique and challenge it.

Trinitarian doctrine also exemplifies this in its tendency to theological historicization (especially in eschatology). In particular it has accepted the immanentism of a largely uncritical linear narrative structure. Moltmann is again cited. Moltmann uses Joachim's trinitarian view of history as a way of unifying Augustine's supposed dualism of kingdoms. That is, he brings processes of redemption and consummation all into history by historicizing them sequentially. The complaint here again is theological impoverishment, a dilution of full trinitarianism, because the age of the Spirit eventually

---

[61] Ibid., p. 123.
[62] Fletcher quotes Hannah Arendt approvingly: 'Since we have made life our supreme and foremost concern we have no room left for an activity based on contempt for one's own self-interest': Fletcher, *Disciplining the Divine*, p. 130, quoting Hannah Arendt, *Between Past and Future* (London: Faber & Faber, 1961, pp. 52–3).
[63] Even Colin Gunton is cited as an example, in Colin Gunton, *The Promise of Trinitarian Theology* (Edinburgh: T & T Clark, 1991).

overcomes the age of Father and Son.[64] The sequential frame also has the effect of implying movement towards a single final unifying goal (in history), which therefore flattens the reality of multiple histories, each with their own integrity. Here Fletcher is echoing Miroslav Volf's critique of Moltmann; Volf dismisses any historical 'completion' of history because it ignores the reality of the 'wreckage' of history which such a (temporal) end would not redeem.[65]

These are sharp polemics, and they may not all convince. Yet the main point is powerfully demonstrated. Historical narrative may be necessary but it is not sufficient; a transcendent source of meaning which supervenes across linear structures also matters. All this echoes much of what I have been arguing.

Moreover, when it comes to Fletcher's own constructive proposals there is a further support in an even more direct way. For these also gesture at precisely the kind of radical transcendence of time which I have been proposing. This might seem counter-intuitive since one of Fletcher's concerns was to construct a particular kind of political and social theology *in history* (i.e. one which has sufficient teeth to bite the cultural hand that has fed it and challenge a political status quo). But in fact his point was precisely that only a transcendent source of meaning can achieve this.[66] Thus he points to 'eternal' moments which relate to time but which seem to transcend time: like the 'winks and blinks, play and orgasms' of our experience there are 'traces of the experience of a temporality that is resolutely other-than-historical time and which, because of their nature, tend to elude history [that is, historical process] as purpose'.[67] Only these instants can be radically transformative of history, precisely because they come from beyond the normal linear patterns of history.

---

[64] 'What Moltmann fails to mention … is that in Joachim's schema we are beseeched to look towards the overcoming of Christ *historically* in terms of the goal of history itself, the Holy Spirit. Thus the Trinity is actually relativised and, indeed, divided – historically. The age of the Father and the age of the Son are overtaken historically in a qualitatively new, transcending temporality of the Spirit. The Trinity is flattened and history is deified'. Fletcher, *Disciplining the Divine*, p. 138.

[65] In fact Volf's own final vision of the redemption of history is not exempt from criticism either. Fletcher finds it hard to see how it shapes social practices in a way that distinguishes from the agenda of immanent liberal social values. The full critical edge of a transcendent source of meaning seems compromised here too. Fletcher actually criticizes Barth at this point as well. In Fletcher's view Barth still creates space for the process of over-historicization by his insistence on dialectic (rather than *analogia entis*), and by his insistence that reconciliation is foregrounded, leaving the importance of final ('eternal') redemption too much in the background.

[66] This resonates with Barth's concerns in his rejection of natural theology, and also nicely demonstrates the irony in refusing to appeal to transcendent meaning for the sake of being effective in public theology!

[67] Fletcher, *Disciplining the Divine*, p. 160.

Kiekegaard is influential here, although too subjective in his grasp of such instants for Fletcher's taste. Barth also springs to mind, certainly the early Barth of the *Epistle to the Romans*. There he identifies a point which is no movement *in* time but 'between times': a moment, therefore, where 'the prevailing accommodation of modern Christianity with history is overwhelmed by the irruption of another time' which has a 'non-sequential character' and enables us to think 'outside and ahead of' historicized eschatologies.[68]

In any case, whatever his sources, Fletcher's outcome clearly resonates. These supervening 'between' times which re-frame events are what a re-imagined providence needs from transcendence. What Fletcher gestures to here is not a fully formed theology. It was, inevitably, unfinished work. Nonetheless the heart of it is clear enough. It is a theology which refused to find meaning only in historical process, even though always related to history.[69] It is above all an unashamed and robust appeal to the sort of categories of transcendence which are necessary to support the meaning of providence being re-imagined.

In summary

What then does all this re-imagining amount to? Not a single, fully formed, doctrine of providence. It is more a collage of conceptual and empirical possibilities. But, as such, at least it shows there are still ways of conceiving divine purposive causality, both within and beyond the temporal order. It shows there are still ways of imagining events to have meaning beyond the meaning we impose on them ourselves. It also shows there are ways of configuring actual empirical events to support that transcendent meaning, while still respecting their integrity. None of these ways may be individually compelling. They are only possibilities. Nevertheless, taken together, I suggest they can and do support a real shape and substance to re-imagined providence.

---

[68] Ibid., pp. 161–2.

[69] Fletcher summarizes thus: 'by attending to the significance of this crossing of time and eternity we can see how it is that, *pace* Moltmann and Volf and those eschatological theologians for whom the future is everything, the character of a paroxysmal, resistant time is *never straightforwardly teleological or rhythmic*, oscillating and vacillating amid discord and resolution. Its generative principle is an intensity, an energy, a dynamic that opens up a stage upon which to perform ... a mode of enactment [which is] not excited by the to and fro of dialectical fluctuation between history and its end'. Ibid., p. 168 (emphasis mine).

This is only a shadowy shape. It does not rest on particular signs or interventions which impose a meaning on everything by their unique causal strangeness; on the contrary, it is shaped by an invisible, transcendent, causation. Nor is it normally evident in big linear stories of history: it certainly does not emerge as one story of unequivocal progress where the sequence moves in clear linear progression towards a single goal; its meaning emerges instead only through the very particular shape of the pivotal redemptive event of Christ, and then a largely hidden joining of instants and small scattered stories with him, in which that shape is echoed and repeated.

Nonetheless, precisely in that pivotal shape of redemption in the Christ event, there *is* real meaning to be found. And this meaning will be specifically identifiable in at least some other events too, especially when figurally grasped. Moreover, *all* events can be imagined with this meaning in principle – especially when supported by a properly imagined notion of radical transcendence.

Such is the sort of providence which I believe can be affirmed as a universal reality. Such is the reason why the instinct for metanarrative, however hidden and unfashionable, is so enduring. And such is the reason behind that persisting sense of presence and purpose in the world which haunts so pervasively, even when it seems absent.

5

Credibility in Scripture, Experience and Praxis

Thus a particular experience persists. The theological form of it proves especially enduring because under pressure it can always be reconfigured. New theological imaginings of it can and do develop. That has been the story so far.

And we could leave it there. But it still needs some more, final, testing. For in the end the theological credibility of what has emerged in these new imaginings will depend on their roots, not just on the fact of their development. In other words, it will depend on whether what has emerged is convincingly displayed in scripture, experience, praxis, not just in abstracted theological reflection itself.

This final chapter therefore recapitulates in just these terms. First by reference back to scripture. Does this emerging shape of providence still authentically express those biblical roots outlined at the outset? Then by referral to experience. How realistic does this providence look both in ordinary life, and in the extremes of human experience? Finally by reflection on Christian praxis. How convincingly is it displayed there? Most of these issues have already been touched on in some way. What follows attempts to draw out these threads only a little further. But in this way the overall theological picture which has been developed should, I hope, be at least a little more grounded – and credible.

Scripture

So far as scripture is concerned I believe this theological picture has remained manifestly well grounded. This is particularly clear in its overall balance. This reshaping of providence has combined ultimate metanarrative, apophaticism and the importance of particularity, all pivoted crucially on the Christ narrative. On almost any hermeneutical basis, these are exactly scripture's own balance of ingredients. Provided we are willing to make generalizations, this is easily demonstrated.

Thus to begin with, scripture clearly has the sense of ultimate metanarrative. God has a plan to 'unite all things in heaven and earth'. God is represented as a personal agent working purposively as source, guide and goal of all that is. God (in Christ) is represented as 'holding all things together' and 'reconciling all things'.[1] This is clearly presented as a belief about God's covenant with creation as a whole, and God's act of redemption for the whole. For although displayed through specific histories and sub-narratives, these are also always given wider, connected, significance. This is especially evident in the way Paul narrates the relation of Jewish and Gentile stories. They may seem to be separate, but they are also ultimately connected, grafted into 'one vine', which issues finally in the unity of all things (Rom. 9–11).

At the same time there is an essential mystery about this metanarrative, so scripture is also partly apophatic. This is very evident in sub-narratives where individuals are sometimes reduced to incomprehension and silence (like Job). But it is also true of the metanarrative itself – where, for example, the Pauline proposal of an overall story of collective Jewish-Christian history asserts meaning but still admits mystery; in spite of its confident assertion about some final unity, there is no sense of *how* that final unity of purpose will actually embrace 'all things' and all stories; instead, God's judgements are 'unsearchable', God's ways are 'inscrutable'.

Equally, in places where purpose and meaning are specifically identified in scripture, particularity is always displayed. Throughout scripture the wider meaning of any event is characteristically given through its figural relation to a particular story, rather than through reference to any overall ideology. In the first instance this is the story of the people of Israel, then it is the pivotal story of Christ himself. He is shown to be the ultimate basis for identifying these figural relations, as well as for asserting an overall final unity. Hence Paul's repeated *en Christo*, and the Johanine 'word made flesh'. Here we see God giving shape to all history, global or personal, not by imposing abstract principle but through the particularity of the Christ event.

---

[1] Cf. Eph. 3; Rom. 11; Col. 1.

This importance of particularity is also present in scripture in more specific ways. It can be seen in the specific narrative structure of the events of Christ's life, which focuses on the particular culminating events of his death and resurrection. The concentration of meaning there follows from the literary genre in which the Gospels were written (comparable to Graeco-Roman 'bios'). It is a kind of biography which does not give much detail about the whole life, but deliberately centres on those particular climactic events of its hero's life and death, and in the case of Christ, what followed his death.[2]

The actual meaning we find in those culminating events then refers us back again to that same overall balance of metanarrative and apophaticism. For what we see in the death and resurrection is precisely the co-existence of a definitive redemptive purpose with bewilderment, apparent failure and even death; the co-existence of a story which includes resurrection and reconciliation with a cry of dereliction and a band of followers who deserted, lost heart, lost their way.[3] As such it is particularly clear here how a providential doctrine of God's hidden purposes being found through evil and emptiness is not just a later theological device or invention of late modernity – it is thoroughly grounded in the particularities of scripture itself.

Another developed feature of providence resonating well with scripture is its wariness about linear progress. What emerged in our theology was a providence of figurally and sychronically grasped meanings and purpose, not just chronologically grasped linear readings. This too has clearly derived from scripture. For the meaning we find in the scriptural narrative of the Christ event does not unfold in a straightforward linear sequence. It is not simply a sequence of moments, one leading to the next and leaving the former behind, the good always following the bad and supplanting it.

---

[2] Cf. Richard Burridge, *What are the Gospels? A Comparison with Graeco-Roman Biography* (2nd edn, Grand Rapids: Eerdmans, 2004).

[3] To be clear: this does not mean scripture portrays a theology in which death, failure, betrayal, are in themselves as an intended purpose of God, nor even a specifically intended instrument of good purpose. On the contrary, Pauline theology insists that death is an 'enemy' and sin must *not* be endorsed 'so that grace may all the more abound'. What the structure of the christological centre shows is, rather, that the deaths, disasters, dead ends and bewilderments of this contingent world are made to *connect* with divine purpose, not to be its object. As such, the elements of bewilderment and pain are integral within the realization of the purpose. But they are not instrumentalized as a specific intention. This too is entirely commensurate with the theology of providence being proposed. See further below, pp. 149–53.

Superficially it might seem so, since the resurrection followed the death. But in fact the event is presented much more as a whole where the good and bad appear together. Like a symphony it has different movements woven together synchronically as well as diachronically.[4] John's Gospel, for example, is especially clear that the glory is not just in the resurrection *after* the cross but somehow contained contemporaneously *with* it; likewise, the Spirit who comes 'after' both events is also the Spirit of Christ who points 'back' to Christ crucified as if there too.

This pattern is replicated elsewhere more generally in scripture. In all the stories of creation, election and new covenant, there is no simple and inexorable progress from darkness to light, from nothingness to fruitfulness, from death to life. Instead, many moments of creation, fall and redemption *co*-exist and recapitulate each other.

Such an attitude to progress in history is well displayed in the answer scripture gives to one of its own rhetorical questions. The Gospel poses the question: when the Son of Man returns 'will He find faith everywhere on earth?'[5] Put another way, when history is finally wound up, will he find a triumphant and faithful church and good order ruling the world as a visible end point of progress, the fruit of the whole process? The clear scriptural answer implied here is no! What he will find at the end will be faith hidden and scattered amongst the continuing divisions, wars, rumours of wars. He will find it as we find the mixed wheat and tares of the parable, allowed to grow together. In other words, what he will find and come to gather into eternity is not some clear end point to which we have all progressed: what he will gather up will come from many moments and stories of faith and goodness wherever they occurred throughout history, whether or not such faith seem to have contributed to any connected line of 'progress', regardless of their link to evil and failure, whether or not they have already faded into oblivion in terms of the world's remembered history. So it is in this way – in the continual generation of mixed and often fleeting moments of faith and goodness, rather than in a visibly connected progress – that the kingdom keeps unfolding. This, I suggest, is the pattern pre-eminently displayed in the culminating events of

---

[4]   Cf. Oliver O'Donovan, *The Desire of the Nations* (Cambridge: Cambridge University Press, 1996), for example, p. 161.

[5]   Lk. 18.8.

Jesus life and death, and echoed in his teaching.[6] And as such it is displaying exactly the sort of picture that the figural readings of providence have been conveying.

Finally, there is the theme of radical transcendence. This too is manifestly displayed in scripture, just as it was a vital ingredient of our theology. It is evident especially in the recurring biblical notion of a final gathering and fulfilment. For in both apocalyptic and Pauline literature the notion of a final general resurrection involves a transformation of experience which demands radically new categories: that is, it implies a radically transcendent kind of place and time where all who have occupied narratives of ordinary time, at any point within that linear framework, may be raised and transformed. In other words, the new heaven and new earth in which all this history is transformed is an imagined *eternity*, not just a further narrative of fulfilment tacked on to the end of ordinary time. It exists as a different kind of reality alongside temporal reality, not just coming after it. That is why God is described as God of the (already) living, when designated as the God of the ('dead') Abraham, Isaac and Jacob. This reading of biblical eschatologies will not be accepted by all. But it is, I believe, necessary.[7] And as such, scripture is readily displaying exactly the sort of transcendence implied in our theological 'construct'.

In these ways, then, scripture and theology remain fully consonant. In both we find a providence and eschatology which is uncompromising in its affirmation of God's purpose 'to unite all things in heaven and earth' – an effective purpose underwritten both by a universal scope of divine activity in history and a radically transcendent place of fulfilment beyond history. Equally in both, we do not find it readily; it is not evident in one continuous stream of

---

[6]   Jesus's parables of the kingdom – the seed sown in the field, the mustard seed, the leaven in the bread – are often called parables of growth, but that is misleading: contemporary hearers will easily project onto them secular ideas of growth *as* progress or historical development, whereas in fact they show just this same pattern: that is, a kingdom already present but often in the small and buried, not just in some the universal and visible end point; and a connection between the hidden seed and the full harvest which is *not* linear, obvious, empirically trackable like the outcome of some inevitable evolutionary development. Instead, the connection between seed and full harvest for the Palestinian would have been the mysterious, unchartable, apparently random, because created by God's unique power to give life. Cf. Richard Bauckham and Trevor Hart, *Hope Against Hope* (London: Darton, Longman & Todd, 1999).

[7]   Thus I take a different view here to N. T. Wright in *The Resurrection of the Son of God* (London: SPCK, 2004). Wright sees time and narrative still defining the new heaven and new earth more univocally: his adherence to the Hebraic roots of scripture makes him wary of the more radical view of eternity – but see my discussion of this in Vernon White, *Life Beyond Death* (London: Darton, Longman & Todd, 2006), especially chs 3 and 4.

history moving inexorably to one end in a self-evident linear pattern of progress, but more opaquely. Yet also in both we *can* still find it, especially in particular stories: particular places where Christ is figurally displayed, as present signs of the ultimate shape of the kingdom not yet seen everywhere. In short, in both scripture and theology we find history neither progressing nor merely repeating itself, but we do sometimes see it 'rhyming'[8] – and it is those christological rhymes which will ultimately prove to be the shape of everything.

General experience

I also believe the account of providence offered here matches well with experience. As with scripture, 'experience' is broad category with a huge hinterland of hermeneutics. But again, if we are prepared to make generalizations, real points of connection are there to be made.

The mapping of our earlier chapters can help here. The intellectual history of purpose and the literary search for it can serve as reflective summaries of experience. And they both revealed paradoxes of experience which map very readily onto our theology. Thus on the one hand we saw a stream of persistent, positive experience about objective purpose, in both reflective thought and in literary reflection, still pervasive even in the context of an increasingly godless world. So even when we took soundings in the worlds of Hardy and Barnes – where a sense of divine purpose was, so to speak, tested to destruction – the residual sense of it has remained, at least in a few particular moments. On the other hand we also saw the manifest experience of its absence – a growing strand of experience, especially from modernity onwards, in which purpose seems only to exist as subjectivity, a self-creation.

This paradox is exactly what has been displayed in our theological picture. It is entirely consonant with a providential theology which asserts a sovereign will of God, but whose words, concepts and judgements about it in particular events can often only 'slip, slide, perish' into apophaticism. It fits well with a theology in which a wider transcendent reference for meaning is always

8 A quotation attributed to Mark Twain: 'History doesn't repeat itself but it does rhyme.'

required, and where particular moments of experience and smaller stories are often the only route to grasping it.

The same sort of judgement can be made when we look at specifically Christian experience. There we find a similar texture, a paradox of purpose and perplexity. *Prima facie* this might seem odd. Faith might be expected to give more substance to our sense of purpose. A faith conviction in God as a personal agent, sustained within the collective reinforcement of a faith community, might be expected to give the committed Christian a very different kind of experience. But not so. Christian experience is not so privileged. It is not exempt from the same paradoxes. For in fact any faith in a sovereign, Christlike, transcendent God, sets the bar so high for the principle of divine purpose (i.e. as a *good* purpose in *all* events) that it creates its own new form of bewilderments – as well as new assurances.

We caught sight of this in Barth. At the centre of expounding his theology of the hidden lordship of God he offers this extraordinary aside specifically about Christian experience:

> This providence and lordship affect [the Christian] as they do all other creatures … he participates in them differently … from within … having a kind of 'understanding' – if we may put it in this way – with the overruling God. … [However] in practice … he is faced every day afresh with riddles of the world process, with the precipices and plains, the blinding lights and obscurities, of the general creaturely occurrence to which his own life's history also belongs. He can only keep asking: Whence? And Whither? And Why? And Wherefore? Of course he has no master-key to all the mysteries of the great process of existence as they crowd in upon him every moment in a new form, to all the mysteries of his own existence as a constituent existence in the historical process of all created reality. On the contrary, he will be the one man who knows that there is no value in any of the master-keys which man has thought to discover and possess. He is the one who will always be most surprised, the most affected, the most apprehensive and the most joyful in the face of events. He will not be like an ant which has foreseen everything in advance, but like a child in a forest, or on Christmas Eve; one who is always rightly astonished by events, by the encounters and experiences which overtake him and the cares and duties laid upon him. He is the one who is constantly forced to begin afresh, wrestling with the possibilities which open out to him and the impossibilities which oppose him. If we may put it this way, life in the world, with all its joys and sorrows

and contemplation and activity, will always be for him a really interesting matter, or, to use a bolder expression, it will be an adventure, for which he for his part has ultimately and basically no qualifications. ...[9]

This is a fine statement of the similarities of faith experience to 'ordinary' experience. Belief in a divine metanarrative at work confers no immunity from bewilderment. Events still surprise. The Christian is still apprehensive. Apparent impossibilities will still arise. To this extent the Christian life is an experience like everyone else's. It is an arena in which we may dimly sense an overall objective purpose, but still find ourselves having to create only our own limited and proximate meanings and purposes. So it fits well with what any theology with an apophatic element is expressing. It is just what we might expect from a divine sovereignty whose final resolutions have to remain in the transcendent realm.

To be sure, this does not rule out some differences in Christian experience as well. Barth describes the texture of what life throws at us to be sometimes more like an 'adventure' and 'interest' for the Christian. This too matches our theology well. After all, we have to reckon that the reality of a divine transcendent action and purpose, however opaque, will at least provide the possibility we can always find meaning. It will be able to freight otherwise pointless events with *some* sense of meaning, even if much of it remains hidden and deferred. It may also mean we sometimes experience specific revelations of God. That is clearly compatible with a radically transcendent, free, 'untamed' God, who may well choose to be more luminous in some particular events and particular moments.[10]

Even so, the point remains that even these transformed moments would still be part of a paradoxical experience. As Barth has also put it, we still cannot

---

[9] Barth, *CD* 111/3, pp. 242–3.

[10] The transcendence of God has often been both conceptually and experientially linked with intense revelation. It was, for example, just this sense of 'wildness' in God, especially in the operation of grace, which offered Placher the metaphor for his own treatise on radical transcendence. He cites the case of the seventeenth-century theological teacher Anne Hutchinson. She was exiled from the Massachusetts Bay Colony for proposing the sort of unpredictable doctrine of love and grace that might threaten social order. It is, for Placher, an apt illustration of how seventeenth-century theology generally tried (wrongly) to tame and domesticate the meaning and experience of God. In other words, a proper grasp of the freedom of radically transcendent God finds credibility just as much in the wildness of experience as in ordered systems which suppress it. C. S. Lewis gave literary form to much the same point in his imaginative representation of a Christ-figure as a Lion: specifically, 'not a tame Lion'! Cf. Placher, *The Domestication of Transcendence*.

and do not easily find in them a decisive or universal 'master-key' or overall pattern. That always remains beyond our experience – and that is again just what a properly transcendent theology would lead us to expect, for a Christian as much as for anyone else.

Of course, a full exploration of Christian experience requires much more than this. It would need mapping through biographies, liturgies and devotional literature as well as more theology, much more than I can offer here. Nonetheless, I'm confident that it would, overall, still yield this same picture. On the one hand we will find records of experience which bewilder; on the other hand particular experiences *may* sometimes illuminate. Perplexity and the sense of purpose always coinhere; bafflement and excitement always co-exist. This is the balance written through almost all biography, whether secular or Christian. And it certainly fits our figural theology of providence. This too, as we saw throughout, has offered no unrealistic short-cut to serenity, conveyed no offer of being a master map-reader of God's ways, yet it does still recognize that there is deep meaning and purpose in particular events.

In short, this theology finds itself well grounded in both secular and sacred experience, at least in general terms. From unfaith and faith, from Barnes to Barth, the textures and paradoxes of experience are well accommodated in a doctrine of providence which relies so much on figural shapes and hidden meanings.

The extremes of experience

But what of those experiences which seem flatly to refuse all meaning, even deferred meaning? I do not need to spell them out again. There are surd and evil experiences, on a global or individual scale, which are not merely perplexing but an outrage against all sense, especially moral sense. Can even these be credibly matched, in any sense, with this theology?

The short answer may simply have to be no. There is no interpretation, no theological justification, that will satisfy – not in this life and our current frame of reference. Theology may just have to accept its limits here. Yet even here theology can at least clarify itself. It can try to make clear what it is and is not asking us to believe, even if it does not always seem believable. Drawing on threads already covered I will therefore attempt at least that sort of clarification.[11]

To begin with, we can be clear that this theological picture of God's purposes involves believing that good meaning really can be brought out of *all* events. This is an inescapable implication in any picture where God's sovereign will foresees all that happens, permits all that happens to happen, and is involved in all that happens by actively relating all that happens to a wider (hidden) context where it is redeemable. We can also be clear this means that God, as universal agent, is specifically in an agent's relation to all events – and this must hold for events of human and natural evil. As such, on some philosophical and legal definitions of agency, that also means we have to say God has some responsibility for these events.[12] Although sometimes desperately hard to accept, this must be the clear implication of any theology of God's purpose and providence which is built on this belief in radical divine agency and sovereignty, based on the Christ event.[13]

However, we also need to be clear this does not require us to believe God *intends* any evil event in itself. That is because what God intends is always the wider context of meaning, not any evil event 'in itself'.[14] This is an important distinction – one we saw that Calvin made, and Barth implied when he insisted on God's will for the recapitulation and redemption of every particular.

We should also be clear what this wider (transcendent) context of redemption which God intends actually is: it is a state in which good is created out of evil events for the benefit of those who suffered the evil (i.e. an internal relation), not just for the good of others (an external relation). In other words, what God intends is a context of redemption whereby evil is transformed not just outweighed or compensated. So it is always transformed evil which God intends, not the evil involved in the process.[15]

---

[11] I am well aware that the way I express what follows may not satisfy some requirements of modal logic. I take the view here, however, that to attempt to defend in it in those terms would simply obfuscate, not clarify, for most readers.

[12] Cf. White, *The Fall of a Sparrow*, ch. 5.

[13] It is important to note this is an implication of radical sovereignty as displayed in the actual narrative of the Christ event, not just as an abstract principle.

[14] The notion of an event 'in itself' is itself elusive. See further in White, *The Fall of a Sparrow*, pp. 123ff.

[15] See pp. 134–5 above.

Of course, whether such transformations are actually credible in experience is another matter. Although we might sometimes see it happen in some events (e.g. we sometimes see how the bitterness of a rupture in a personal relationship is made into the particular sweetness of reconciliation), we might never be able to see this pattern in some other events, not in this life. But then remember – the point here is not to argue for the credibility of this picture in all experience: I am simply trying to clarify what the picture must entail.[16]

Another clarification follows if we ask whether this picture means we are being asked to believe that it is 'all worth it' – for all concerned. Here the answer again has to be yes. That is the clear implication of such a universal redemptive process of transformation. On the other hand, it does *not* necessarily mean it is the best of all possible worlds in every particular. That is because although every event and sub-narrative is redeemable into a good purpose, none is in itself necessary to those purposes. Others might have occurred. It is true we have portrayed the eternal God foreseeing and permitting all actual sub-plots which contingency and creaturely acts generate, and then acting redemptively in relation to them. But this does not confer any absolute necessity on them, as if any one of them is specifically God's essential 'policy'.[17] The only kind of necessity here lies in their redeemed *outcome* in the wider context of eternity – and that is a necessity derived from the freedom and love of God rather than any other metaphysical necessity.

This last point then clarifies further. For this divine necessity to transform, which might seem to derive chiefly from the demands of divine sovereignty, is actually driven primarily by a radical view of divine love. That is because the sovereign scope of divine action which 'must' relate God to all things (including evil) is itself the outcome of love. Put another way, love is the primary motivating disposition of all divine action; sovereign power just brings it into effect, and ensures that it is responsible love.

---

[16] For more extended discussion see White, *The Fall of a Sparrow*, ch. 7.

[17] Cf. Rowan Williams, 'Redeeming Sorrows: Marilyn McCord Adams and the Defeat of Evil', in M. Higton (ed.), *Wrestling with Angels: Conversations in Modern Theology* (London: SCM Press, 2007), pp. 255–74. Williams adopts a kind of neo-Thomist view of divine action in which timelessly ordered systems are sustained in history by God. Particular configurations within that may then be expressive of God's will in particular ways, but as such they are 'foreordained results of finite outcomes' not specific policies of God. Williams' primary aim here is to counter both a merely reactive view of God's plans, which he finds in Wiles, as well as an interventionist God competing with finite causes.

Radical sovereign power and radical (responsible) love are therefore shown here to be inextricably related to each other. All creative endeavour of love which is meant by God in any effectual sense (including Williams's semiotic sense) would be grossly irresponsible if its risks were not recoverable by sufficient sovereign power. To create processes of sentient life but then be unable to steer them to an ultimate good end, except through sacrificing or instrumentalizing them, would fatally compromise the agent's love.[18] That is why responsible creative love and sovereign efficacy can never be traded off against each other. It is all of a piece with how universal and transcendent agency operates generally: that is, it is able effectively to incorporate the creature's own causality to bring it to its ultimate good end, but without overwhelming or coercing. This is exactly the sort of love and power displayed in the narratives of Christ and the kingdom of God, where power does not displace love and freedom but nonetheless works through it effectively.

This clarifies further not least because it helps distinguish this account from many others which operate with a form of limited sovereignty or competitive causality; that is, accounts where God's purposes are ultimately subject to risks. These accounts have a fundamentally different logic. Ostensibly they rescue God from the charge of immediate responsibility and direct involvement in evil. But in fact they have to face their own crisis of credibility. For what value is the sincere intention of creative love in God's continuing creation if there is no assurance of ultimate good outcome for any particular creature? Without the resource of radical sovereignty the creative act actually becomes a source of fear, not of gratitude.

There is an irony here which needs noting. A more vulnerable God, conceived within a metaphysics of reciprocal being and causality, is often proposed to make God more accessible and personal. But in fact it removes all real relationship of trust – for God has become a God who has brought us into being without being able to fulfil love effectively. In short, the real terror is not of a sovereign God but an impotent one. So at this stark point of choice I know that if I believe anything I must choose to believe the sovereign God rather than the impotent God – precisely in order to believe in the real love of God.

---

[18] Again, for more extended discussion of this see White, *The Fall of a Sparrow*, pp. 86–93; also Vernon White, *Paying Attention to People: An Essay on Individualism and Christian Belief* (London: SPCK, 1996), ch. 9.

Such, then, is the nature of the theology offered here when faced with the extremes of experience. I should say again that this is not meant as a claim to theodicy. It is not a theology to satisfy or explain all our experience. It is just an attempt to clarify its own meaning. The judgement whether that meaning makes it any more or less credible can then be made – either way. But at least we can make that judgement more honestly if we know what we are judging.

Praxis: Prayer, social action, public movements

Then finally there is the matter of praxis. Does this theology also have credibility *in action*? In general terms, yes. This has been a theology where human purposive action has been consistently incorporated within divine action and purpose, not displaced by it. Even Calvin allowed it some meaning; and this developing theological picture has assumed much more. It is (in Quash's terms) a theology which while 'honouring the Calvinist concern to prioritize divine initiative and make God's action the embracing context of all human action' also 'makes human intendings and wishings into integral moments within a divine framework'.[19] However – can we also now ground this more concretely? Can we show how this theology also maps onto specific things we actually do? Can we also show how it functions normatively, guiding the things we ought to do?

I think we can. Christian communities and individuals, as a matter of fact, do practise some sort of belief in providence – and providence can, at best, act normatively to guide them. For a start, there is simply the existence of what we might describe as a 'called' community. That is to say, there are communities of faith which imply a broadly Christian providential belief simply because they claim to be responding to purposes given by a personal God, as distinct from appealing to any other agency. In this general sense every movement of church history is concrete evidence of some sort of implicit providential belief.

This becomes more specifically evident in the practice of prayer: that is, when any endeavour is explicitly accompanied by the practice of

---

[19] Cf. Quash, *Found Theology,* p. 48.

prayer – especially prayer for help and 'success' when our goals seem beyond our immediate reach. This sort of prayer is a clear acknowledgement of interrelation and dependence on another agent and that agent's purposes. It does not mean mere acquiescence, quietism or fatalism. After all, the person who prays does not usually shelve projects simply because of belief in a wider divine action which enables them – rather, we assume another agent who incorporates and transforms, rather than replaces, our own action. So in this common practice of prayer providence is actually implied precisely within the nature of human praxis itself – both the prayer and the wider action it accompanies.

Admittedly, not all intercessory prayer has quite this full, nuanced, assumption lying behind it. Some simply expects a miracle: that is, it implies a divine agent who just replaces or overrides ordinary causality. Or else there is prayer which assumes the opposite: it addresses God only as a symbol of aspiration or inspiration; that is, not as another agent at all. So that sort of prayer is entirely self-referential. Nonetheless, much prayer *does* imply a 'proper' providential theology. It is precisely an exercise which acknowledges that what we do is always joined in a transcendent divine action and accommodated within a wider purpose, yet without denying the specificity and integrity of creaturely actions within that transcendent relationship.

It is also a practice consonant with different empirical outcomes of providence. For we continue to act prayerfully whether or not the outcome is luminous. Yes, sometimes a figural connection will light up some prayerful human action as a very clear act of God with a recognizable outcome – but more usually we also have to set out prayerfully to 'serve our community', 'worship God' or 'evangelize the world' without empirical verification of how that meaning is realized. Yet either way, the underlying providential faith is evident. For the presupposition is always that there is another (transcendent) agent making *some* meaning through the prayer.

This sort of praxis also extends beyond the bounds of explicitly prayerful action. All faith-inspired action undertaken with Barth's sense of ultimate hope and adventure, all action predicated on an ultimate meaning or value in life which transcends our own making, is praxis which displays an implicit providential belief. For as such it is, precisely, an action which believes or implies that it is being incorporated in a further 'larger' action, helping to shape events according to this wider purpose. In that sense any prayer which may or may not accompany it is simply making visible an implicit faith of the action itself.[20]

Such praxis may also go beyond any acknowledged religious faith at all. As we saw with the example of Simon Critchley, there is action wholly displaced from conscious theism which nonetheless demonstrates aspects of this sort of belief. There is, for example, the praxis of a sustained political will striving for an immanent end of justice, even when this end is often unattainable empirically in immanent terms.[21] This displays, implicitly, a quasi-transcendent teleological quality to the action: that is, a non-empirical belief is drawing the action forwards. In that sense even an atheist's action can display implicit belief in a sort of secular providence.

To be sure, theologians may remain wary of naming which particular sub-narratives of history can specifically count in this way (i.e. as self-evidently providential), whether faith-inspired or secular. Politicians are similarly cautious, at least in contemporary discourse (both theologians and social commentators were less reticent in the past![22]). Nonetheless the principle remains. A very wide range of public movements of history, whether political, religious or social, can be seen as a display of belief in this sort of implicit providence, theistic or otherwise.

---

[20] Note, however, that prayer can also be believed to be that sort of action *in itself*. That is to say, it can be in itself an action which God incorporates providentially to help shape what happens. Setting aside trivializing pleas for a parking space (poignant, perhaps, as a gesture to 'wild' grace, but crass nonsense when they imply God is pulled arbitrarily into our causal networks just by our wishes!), serious prayer must have this potential. As an authentic meeting for human and divine minds it too has causal potential in the world, as previously argued. Like any other creaturely cause fed into the historical-temporal nexus it can be foreseen and incorporated in some way by God in God's wider context of meaning, whether or not visible within our frame of reference. And as such it displays a belief in providence in itself, just as other faithful actions.

[21] Cf. Critchley, *Infinitely Demanding* (see pp. 32–6 above).

[22] Keith Thomas offers some unfortunate examples from Medieval and Reformation periods in his *Religion and the Decline of Magic*. It was a period when the pitfalls and abuses were all too obvious. Protestants often used God on their side and for their ecclesiastical purposes: so when on 26 October 1623 nearly 100 people were killed when the floor collapsed under the weight of a Roman Catholic congregation in Blackfriars, that was readily interpreted as God's providential judgement. But, just as surely, a Catholic Spanish writer a few years later then noted how God had miraculously spared a Catholic Chapel in the Strand in the Great Fire of London! By contrast, Abraham Lincoln's speech of 4 March 1865 is one of the better examples. He affirmed God's just dealings even through the complex tragedy of the American Civil War where God's providence was invoked on both sides. It is a genuinely nuanced and thoughtful wrestling with providence in relation to specific public events: a rare thing in a politician.

Flawed praxis and the fallacies of 'progress'

Of course, this does not mean that literally all human purposive action is implying the sort of purpose actually being worked out in providence. Not even all action which explicitly predicates itself on providence will do that. Discrimination is needed.

There is, for example, the enfeebled sort of action which claims to 'leave things' to providence simply as a cover for passivity. Or there is the action which claims providence but only to seek grossly perverted ends (Hitler often appealed to providence). These obviously do not match our theology at all. The former because it has made providence complicit with quietism and fatalism, failing to see the transcendent nature of a divine action and purpose which incorporates our action rather than making it redundant. The latter simply because the character and nature of its directing god has been nothing like the Christlike God.

Another flawed form of praxis is that familiar stalking horse for providential praxis which emerges from the ideology of progress. This is often much better intentioned and directed to honourable ends. Yet as a form of action it still does not match this theology we have been exploring – and this needs exposing in more detail, not least because of its plausibility.

I have already noted some of its problematics in principle. Augustine deemed it a danger for ecclesial history because it failed to acknowledge the reality both of flawed human nature and the inscrutable ways of God. Contemporary commentators like Gray have shown why it fails in purely secular terms too. Praxis based on belief in linear progress towards perfection risks disillusionment and demoralization when events do not fall into place. Worse, it risks turning into a self-vindicating attempt to *impose* this order by a forced interpretation of events: that is, ecclesial or political praxis becomes freighted with an exclusive sense of instrumental necessity to 'make' progress happen. The ends are then badly contaminated with the means.

We should now note how these problematics appear in practice too. That is, how frequently church history and political history have actually demonstrated this error in visible ways. So, for example, we could note what happened in the late patristic age when God's master plan for the church was thought to be a straight linear sequence of first suffering, then glory. The consequence when the emperor was converted and martyrdom ceased was to see this as evidence of the plan working: that is, the church came to presume it had reached fulfilment, could take the glory, and rule the world; the church could become the kingdom. But of course, as noted before, Constantinianism was by no means an unqualified success, and the damage then done over centuries in the name of this triumphalist view of religious progress has been immense. With the disruptions of the fall of Rome, schism between East and West, the Reformation and Enlightenment, this flawed theological edifice was then further undermined. By then the full cost of it had been demonstrated. It had left a splintered and discredited church.

Similar consequences can be noted in the various nineteenth-century European temptations to write plans of progress. Evangelical churches of mission proclaimed God's great plan was the proclamation of the Gospel to every nation, which would be the catalyst for the final kingdom to come – so naturally they saw themselves as *the* vital instrument for that to happen. Romantic churches of aesthetic experience, centred in worship, believed God's great plan for the church was ever increasing inward piety and discipline and only that would transform the increasingly squalid urban life of the world – so they naturally saw themselves fulfilling that. Liberal churches saw the master plan as the unfolding of the kingdom through social justice – so naturally saw themselves as key agents for that overall end. However, no simple linear progress actually happened in that way for any of them. The pressure of real events saw to it. Churches of mission and romantic piety were halted by the rise of pluralism and global consumerism. The liberal church of inevitable social progress foundered in the horror of the First World War. In short, as with most great plans, all their assumptions of progress simply fell foul of events in the end. The outcome of predicating praxis on that assumption was, again, disillusionment – and a church still divided.

A parallel story could also be told, as Gray has done, about the dangerous failures of secular programmes. Whenever they have been predicated on an ideology of progress their legacy is flawed. He cites examples from Marxism to unfettered capitalism, through to liberal interventionism. Each has eventually failed in its own terms of success, and so invited disillusionment. Each has also demonstrably (though not equally) exercised forms of instrumental oppression to try to achieve that 'success' – and that too has discredited them.

Back in the ecclesial world the same story could be told about local praxis. Particular churches which have set great theological store on visible growth through ordinary linear time often founder badly if it does not occur – or else adopt more coercive means to make it happen. Either way, spiritual damage is done. This can also be told as a story about individual Christian praxis. Our own personal prayers easily lure us into the same trap. How many have lost all faith because of false expectations of seeing linear 'progress' in the objects of our prayerful longings?

To be clear, none of this means that there are no stories at all of progress in time and history, in either in ecclesial or political spheres. They can indeed occur, in small ways and even in some larger narratives. This is only to be expected with any theology of an effective universal divine purpose at work in history. A divine action working with the universal scope we have imagined, operative at every level of reality, is bound to be empirically identifiable as progress at *some* points.[23] So as we saw in Frei's account, there will at least be some events which can be identified and named as progressing God's will in relative terms.

Yet the important point remains – this sort of progress still cannot be seen as the sole or necessary narrative. What a christological and figural theology describes always requires a much more nuanced account. It means that progressive stories will always co-exist with regressive stories as well. If that is ignored, the assumption of progress in praxis will almost always have this reverse side as well – of coercion, or demoralization.[24] That is why the praxis of pure progress, although seductive, is always flawed.

Purpose without progress

The proper form of providential praxis, by contrast, now becomes even more apparent. Over against these aberrations its authentic shape emerges more clearly. It will be precisely that praxis which pursues purpose *without*

---

[23] Cf. Pinker, *The Better Angels of our Nature*. Pinker offers an empirically and statistically based argument for a long-term decline in socially approved violence, since the Enlightenment.

[24] So there are obvious qualifications to Pinker's thesis the moment it becomes an ideology. See, for example, Leah Bradshaw, 'Are We Getting Better? A Review of Pinker's *The Better Angels of our Nature*', anamnesis.journal.com/2013/11steven-pinker-better-angels-of-our-nature.

the necessity of visible, linear, progress.[25] It will be the sort of action which embraces the complexity of apparent success and apparent failure. It will be action following a figural pattern, finding its meaning in particulars and in substreams of events when it cannot find it in the big story.

As such, it will have particular characteristics. For example, since we do not pursue purpose just in the hope of long linear temporal, connections, we will find meaning just as much in action with 'vertical' dimensions. In other words, we will pursue action whose meaning will sometimes lie in a depth of a present experience rather than discernible future outcomes, action which connects with eternity as much as temporal history. Such vertical meanings are characteristically best displayed in human relationships. There we can find purpose in individual acts of generosity with other people (including strangers), whether or not this connects with any visible long-term achievement. In such personal acts we can find purpose and joy at the time even though it may appear fruitless if measured by its consequences the next day – because we know it has connected with eternal not just temporal meaning (the Gospel story of a woman's gift of costly ointment springs to mind).

By the same token it will be a praxis which can also find meaning 'laterally', in loose associations with other events, again rather than in straightforward linear progression. This is often best displayed in community enterprises. There are numerous collective efforts which seem to fail in their linear trajectory but catch fire laterally in some other place and time (here a particular transplanted youth club in north London springs to mind).

Connected with this is the capacity generally to find meaning in action within particular sub-narratives without needing to subsume these within some known wider metanarrative. In a figural construction of meaning God does not need to join up all our projects into one metanarrative in order to make meaning from them – so neither do we. They can serve God's meaning as separate sub-narratives.

On a large scale this means, for example, that a political praxis leading to the spread of democracy and human rights might well be celebrated as part of

---

[25] Cf. Quash, citing Hardy in *Found Theology*, p. 286: 'A movement which may not be linear, will not always be progress' yet which is still 'useful for God's purposes'. Cf. D. Hardy, D. Ford, P. Ochs and D. F. Ford, *Wording a Radiance: Parting Conversations on God and Church* (London: SCM Press, 2010).

providence at work – *but* without any need to proclaim it as an overall master plan of God into which all other political histories must be fitted and joined. A proper praxis will let these other stories stand alongside each other, rather than skew or devalue them in the name of linear progress by trying to fit them into one overall master plan of Western democracy (or any other). Likewise with church history: the various movements of ecclesial reform may all display some meaning, but our particular praxis will serve this best by honouring them in their own right, not trying to divert or dilute them into one great rolling river (an ultimate end and connection which lies beyond our grasp anyway).

In all this it is clear that this kind of action can be sustained whatever its visible outcome. It will be able to withstand both the rise and fall of apparent success that future events will bring. If there is 'success' this can be greeted without triumphalism because we know this one narrative is not the only way God makes meaning. If there is apparent failure this can be greeted without despair for the same reason. In the same way this sort of action can also be deeply motivated yet without the tyranny of absolutism. Believing that all our actions can all be joined with a hidden divine purpose is uniquely inspirational – that is the motivation. Yet precisely because it is joined to overall purposes other and bigger than ours, it must also recognize its own contingency – that is why it cannot take itself as absolute even though it serves an absolute end.

In short, this will be an irrepressible kind of action, but uniquely yoked with humility and realism; it will be joyful, but will never be just a facile optimism; it need never despair, but neither can it claim any triumphalism. It is very different from a discipleship fired only by a superficial providence, or wedded to a secular myth of progress – which all too easily defaults to arrogance when progress happens and all too easily falters or fails when progress does not happen. It is an overall disposition memorably summarized here in this account of a Cambridge resident battling the 1952 Fenland floods: 'It's like in the floods … a sandbag team toiled all day and seemed to have succeeded. Then when the last sandbag was placed – the whole dam was swept away. Wasted labour? No! – I don't think so. An eternal building block had still been laid in the City of God.'[26]

---

[26] From a private letter written by C. F. D. Moule. Previously quoted in White, *Life Beyond Death*.

Such is the proper shape of providential praxis. It is a praxis which is both humble and yet thoroughly purposeful. And as such I believe it is particularly important in our current social condition. Humility is always vital. The dangers of arrogance or triumphalism may now be more dormant in Western society generally and especially in mainstream church life, but they can easily erupt again. But persistence and purposefulness is also crucial because, I suggest, there is now as much danger of demoralization as of triumphalism, both in mainstream political culture and ecclesiastical life. Lack of visible progress over many years has been like an internal bleeding in the body.

In these circumstances outright scepticism about providence will not help us act. But nor will a thin theology of progress with trivial and triumphalist slogans seeming to offer much but then dashed by events. Neither will feed either church or society. Only and precisely this richer and thicker theology of a more truly Christ-shaped and figural providence offers a sustainable praxis: one which is realistic, but also confident that God *is* involved in our history, even when events turn against us.

Conclusion: Providence Lost – or Regained?

So where have we arrived in this essay?

A remarkable and persisting sense of purpose has been tracked in general intellectual history, literature and theology. Even apart from theology, we have seen this to be a tradition about transcendence. It has been about a sense of purpose we encounter and do not just construct; about finding a story not just story-making; about an overall purpose which incorporates our own purposes but does not reduce to them. It has been driven by constituent pressures of necessity, narrative and morality, all of which carry their own intrinsic appeal to transcendence, even when displaced from specific religious or metaphysical frameworks. As such this sense of purpose has authority which a purely immanent frame of reference lacks. Any attempt to replace it with merely self-generated purpose proves unsatisfying, leaving 'unease' (Taylor) and 'unrest' (Julian Barnes), not liberation.

When tracked specifically in theology this has became even more apparent. Here too it has been subject to displacing pressures. Scientific causality, historicism, the reality of evil, postmodern scepticism about metanarrative, have all had their effect. But again, it is remarkably persistent. Its constituent drivers here have been belief in divine sovereignty, personal agency, will – the theological counterparts of our more general sense of necessity, narrative and morality. The outcome is continuing significance of a specific doctrine of providence in spite of the pressures on it. Its meaning in big linear stories is no longer easy to identify but it still reappears in particularities, in discrete 'smaller' stories. These still gesture, compellingly, to some wider sense of a transcendent divine purpose. It has been like the bump in a carpet: shifting but obdurate, impossible but necessary, reshaped yet still persisting, and still well grounded in scripture, experience and praxis.

Within this overall trajectory there has nonetheless been loss. We have lost easy ways to identify meaning in particular events. There is no presumption here of special meaning just because events have occurred through unlikely causal means, or just because they had improbable consequences.

This was not always so. In the past, improbable events with momentous outcomes often attracted very confident pronouncements about providence. Whether in Tudor history when historians who favoured Henry VII described the extraordinary circumstances of his accession to the throne, or more recently in the Second World War when the improbable evacuation of troops from Dunkirk kept hope alive, special providence was regularly invoked. But now our theology has lost that kind of certainty. It may live on in personal piety in private interpretations of unusual experiences but there is no clear support in public theology. There is no special significance *just* because there were unlikely means or notable outcomes. Instead, meaning only emerges if we see a figural and Christ-centred interpretation of events – and that is often opaque. It *may* still be found in a public event like Dunkirk, just as it may be found in personal experience: but if so it will relate to some pattern of redemptive Christlike effects in these events, not to their causal complexity or extraordinary outcome. That easy route to providential meaning has now been lost.

There has even been a loss of all sense of meaning, at times. Theology has to accept that some events simply cannot bear the weight of any specific interpretative meanings that we can see within time. Many events remain just as deep perplexities, with entirely hidden meanings. This is not just because they represent gaps in our understanding that we can be sure will be filled later. It is a more radical apophaticism. It is part of our being in time which we have to accept, which we neither can or should escape – until eternity.[1]

Yet, equally, something has certainly been found in this picture too. This theology has clearly reaffirmed the reality of purpose – in everything. Even when its meaning seems impossible to determine in practice, it has refused absolutely to reinterpret objective purpose out of all existence, not even *in extremis*. Instead, it reconstitutes this instinct in a way which tries to make sense of both its absence and presence. It offers a form of providence in which some meaning is given, some deferred, but nothing is finally beyond its reach, because ultimately it reaches into eternity and a transcendent realm.

---

[1] Cf. Urs Von Balthasar who designated it a sin to 'break out of time' prematurely.

As such this is a theology which frees us from the spell of an over-interpreted world but, equally, prevents us from falling under another spell: the lure of complete reductionism and disenchantment. It has resisted the seductive and spurious claim that demystifying is always more honest to 'real' life. On the contrary, it insists that honesty requires willingness to see that reality might include more, not less, than meets the eye of a genuinely open gaze, including purposiveness in improbable places. Thereby this is a theology which will always encourage us to find extraordinary interest in everything. For when God is working purpose out in this much bigger frame, our potential interest in events must also be without limits.

Is this overall a better place to be? I believe so. Providence without any intervening modes of loss has been too thin, and may well not survive the pressures on it. This providence which is reconfigured from loss is surely stronger. Like the shape of water in Rilke's reconstituted fountain, it will not be less real for having decayed in one form before it returns in another. If anything, it is likely to be more real, for it will be less vulnerable to the demolition of false certainties. As Rilke puts it in another poem, 'we are sheltered by our very unprotectedness'.[2]

This, surely, is an authentic mode for any faith and theology. Faith is not secured in static and buffered belief. It subsists in doctrine which is open and dynamic. That, I trust, is what has been offered here: a providence which will not let us go, exactly because it can always be both lost and found.

---

[2] From a poem written in 1924 (discussed by Martin Heidegger in terms of the risk of existence). Good (ed.), *Rilke's Late Poetry*, p. 130.

Select Bibliography

Aquinas, T., *Summa Theologiae* (London: Eyre and Spottiswoode, 1963).

Auerbach, E., *Mimesis: the Representation of Reality in Western Literature* (Princeton: Princeton University Press, 1953/2003).

Augustine of Hippo, *The City of God* (trans. D. Knowles; Harmondsworth: Penguin, 1972).

Augustine of Hippo, *Confessions* (trans. H. Chadwick; Oxford: Oxford University Press, 1992).

Augustine of Hippo, *De Doctrine Christiana* (trans. R. Green; Oxford: Oxford World's Classics, 2008).

Barnes, J., *Metroland* (London: Jonathan Cape, 1980).

Barnes, J., *Flaubert's Parrot* (London: Vintage, 1984/2009).

Barnes, J., *Staring at the Sun* (London: Vintage, 1986/2009).

Barnes, J., *A History of the World in 10 ½ Chapters* (London: Vintage, 1989/2009).

Barnes, J., *The Sense of an Ending* (London: Jonathan Cape, 2011).

Barnes, J., *Levels of Life* (London: Jonathan Cape, 2013).

Barth, K., *Church Dogmatics* III/3 (Edinburgh: T & T Clark, 1976).

Bauckham, R., and Hart, T., *Hope Against Hope* (London: Darton, Longman & Todd, 1999).

Beardslee, W., 'Christ in the Postmodern Age', in D. Griffin (ed.), *Varieties of Postmodern Theology* (Albany: State University of New York Press, 1989), pp. 63–80.

Beer, G., *Darwin's Plots: Evolutionary Narrative in Darwin, George Eliot and Nineteenth-Century Fiction* (Cambridge: Cambridge University Press, 2000).

Bittner, R., 'Augustine's Philosophy of History', in G. Matthews (ed.), *The Augustinian Tradition* (Berkeley: University of California Press, 1999), pp. 345–60.

Brooke, C., 'Grotius, Stoicism and "Oikeiosis"', *Grotiana*, 29 (2008), pp. 25–50.

Burrell, D., *Aquinas, God and Action* (Notre Dame, IN: University of Notre Dame Press, 1979).

Burridge, R., *What are the Gospels? A Comparison with Graeco-Roman Biography* (2nd edn, Grand Rapids: Eerdmans, 2004).

Calvin, J., *Institutes of Christian Religion* (trans. F. Battles; London: Collins, 1986).

Calvin, J., *The Secret Providence of God* (ed. P. Helm; Wheaton, IL: Crossway, 2010).

Cavanaugh, W., 'What Constantine Has to Teach Us', in John Roth (ed.), *Constantine Revisited: Leithart, Yoder and the Constantinian Debate* (Eugene, OR: Wipf & Stock, 2013), pp. 83–99.

Clark, S., *God's World and the Great Awakening* (Oxford: Clarendon Press, 1991).

Clayton, P., and Knapp, S., *The Predicament of Belief* (Oxford: Oxford University Press, 2011).

Coakley, S., 'Evolution, Cooperation, and Divine Providence', in M. Nowak and S. Coakley (eds), *Evolution, Games, and God* (Cambridge, MA: Harvard University Press, 2013), pp. 375–85.

Critchley, S., *Infinitely Demanding: Ethics of Commitment, Politics of Resistance* (London: Verso, 2007).

Critchley, S., *Faith of the Faithless: Experiments in Political Theology* (London: Verso, 2012).

Dawson, J., *Christian Figural Reading and the Fashioning of Identity* (Berkeley: University of California Press, 2002).

Dolezal, J., *God Without Parts: Divine Simplicity and the Metaphysics of God's Absoluteness* (Eugene, OR: Wipf & Stock, 2011).

Eagleton, T., *The English Novel* (Oxford: Blackwell, 2005).

Elliott, M., *Providence Perceived* (New York: De Gruyter, 2015).

Fergusson, D., 'The Theology of Providence', *Theology Today*, 67 (2010), pp. 261–78.

Fiddes, P., *The Creative Suffering of God* (Oxford: Clarendon Press, 1988).

Fletcher, P., *Disciplining the Divine: Towards an (Im)political Theology* (Farnham: Ashgate, 2009).

Flint, T., 'Providence and Predestination', in P. Quinn and C. Taliaferro (eds), *A Companion to Philosophy of Religion* (Oxford: Blackwell, 1997), pp. 569–76.

Frei, H., 'Theological Reflections on the Accounts of Jesus' Death and Resurrection', *Christian Scholar*, 49 (1966), pp. 263–306.

Frei, H., *The Eclipse of Biblical Narrative: A Study in Eighteenth and Nineteenth Century Hermeneutics* (New Haven: Yale University Press, 1974).

Frei, H., *The Identity of Jesus Christ* (Philadelphia: Fortress Press, 1975).

Gatrell, S., *Thomas Hardy and the Proper Study of Mankind* (London: Macmillan, 1993).

Gibson, J. (ed.), *Thomas Hardy: The Complete Poems* (New York: Palgrave, 2001).

Gilkey, L., *Reaping the Whirlwind; A Christian Interpretation of History* (New York: Seabury Press, 1976).

Gillespie, M. A., *The Theological Origins of Modernity* (London: University of Chicago Press, 2008).

Good, G. (trans.), *Rilke's Late Poetry* (Vancouver: Ronsdale Press, 2004).

Gorringe, T., *God's Theatre: A Theology of Providence* (London: SCM Press, 1991).

Gorringe, T., *Karl Barth: Against Hegemony* (Oxford: Oxford University Press, 1999).

Gray, J., *Black Mass: Apocalyptic Religion and the Death of Utopia* (London: Penguin, 2007).

Grenz, S., and Olsen, R., *20th Century Theology: God and the World in a Transitional Age* (Carlisle: Paternoster Press, 1992).

Guignery, V., *The Fiction of Julian Barnes* (Basingstoke: Palgrave Macmillan, 2006).

Hardy, D., *Finding the Church: The Dynamic Truth of Anglicanism* (London: SCM Press, 2001).

Hardy, D., 'Harmony and Mutual Implication in the *Opus Maximum*', in J. Barbeau (ed.), *Coleridge's Assertion of Religion: Essays on the Opus Maximum* (Leuven: Peeters, 2006), pp. 33–52.

Hardy, F., *The Early Life of Thomas Hardy* (London: Macmillan, 1928).

Hardy, T., *Jude the Obscure* (Harmondsworth, Penguin Classics, 1985).

Hardy, T., *The Return of the Native* (Harmondsworth: Penguin Classics, 1985).

Hardy, T., *The Mayor of Casterbridge* (Harmondsworth: Penguin Classics, 1997).

Hardy, T., *Tess of the D'Urbevilles* (Oxford: Oxford World's Classics, 1998).

Hart, D. B., 'Providence and Causality: On Divine Innocence', in F. Murphy and P. Ziegler (eds), *The Providence of God* (London: T & T Clark, 2009), pp. 34–56.

Hebblethwaite, B., *Philosophical Theology and Christian Doctrine* (Oxford: Blackwell, 2005).

Hebblethwaite, B., and Henderson, E. (eds), *Divine Action: Studies inspired by the Philosophical Theology of Austin Farrer* (Edinburgh: T & T Clark, 1990).

Hedley, D., *Living Forms of the Imagination* (London: T & T Clark, 2008).

Higton, M., *Christ, Providence and History: Hans W Frei's Public Theology* (London: T & T Clark, 2004).

Hodgson, P. C., *God in History: Shapes of Freedom* (Minneapolis: Fortress Press, 1989).

Holmes, F., *Julian Barnes* (London: Palgrave Macmillan, 2009).

Horlacher, S., 'Jude the Obscure: From a Metaphysics of Presence to the Blessings of Absence', *Journal of Men, Masculinities and Spirituality*, 1.2 (2007), pp. 116–36.

Kennedy, D., *Providence and Personalism* (Oxford: Peter Lang, 2011).

Kerr, F., *Immortal longings: Versions of Transcending Humanity* (London: SPCK, 1997).

King, R., *The Meaning of God* (London: SCM Press, 1974).

Langford, M., *Providence* (London: SCM Press, 1971).

Lewis, C. S. 'On Stories', in L. Walmsley (ed.), *C. S. Lewis: Essay Collection and Other Short Pieces* (London: HarperCollins, 2000), pp. 491–504.

Lloyd, G., *Providence Lost* (Cambridge, MA: Harvard University Press, 2008).

MacIntyre, A., *After Virtue* (London: Duckworth, 1981).

MacIntyre, A., *Whose Justice? Which Rationality?* (London: Duckworth, 1988).

Muir, E., *Selected Poems* (London: Faber & Faber, 1965).

Murphy, F., and Ziegler, P. (eds), *The Providence of God* (London: T & T Clark, 2009).

O'Donovan, O., *Resurrection and Moral Order* (2nd edn, Leicester: Apollos, 1994).

O'Donovan, O., *The Desire of the Nations* (Cambridge: Cambridge University Press, 1996).

O'Regan, C., 'Hegel, Theodicy and the Invisibility of Waste', in F. Murphy and P. Ziegler (eds), *The Providence of God* (London: T & T Clark, 2009), pp. 75–108.

Paulin, T., *Thomas Hardy: The Poetry of Perception* (London: Macmillan, 1975).

Peacocke, A., *Theology for a Scientific Age* (London: SCM Press, 1993).

Peacocke, A., *All That is: A Naturalistic Faith for the 21st Century* (Minneapolis: Fortress Press, 2007).

Pinker, S., *The Better Angels of our Nature* (London: Allen Lane, 2011).

Placher, W., *The Domestication of Transcendence* (Louisville, KY: Westminster John Knox Press, 1996).

Plant, R., *Politics, Theology and History* (Cambridge: Cambridge University Press, 2001).

Polkinghorne, J., *Exploring Reality: The Intertwining of Science and Religion* (London: Yale University Press, 2005).

Prickett, S., *Narrative, Religion and Science: Fundamentalism versus Irony 1700–1999* (Cambridge: Cambridge University Press, 2002).

Quash, B., *Found Theology: History, Imagination and the Holy Spirit* (London: Bloomsbury, 2013).

Saunders, N., *Divine Action and Modern Science* (Cambridge: Cambridge University Press, 2002).

Sayers, D., *The Mind of the Maker* (London: Victor Gollancz, 1941).

Schleiermacher, F. D. E., *The Christian Faith* (Edinburgh: T & T Clark, 1928).

Schrag, C., *The Self after Postmodernity* (New Haven: Yale University Press, 1997).

Sonderegger, K., 'The Doctrine of Providence', in F. Murphy and P. Ziegler (eds), *The Providence of God* (London: T & T Clark, 2009), pp. 144–57.

Steiner, G., *Real Presences* (Chicago: University of Chicago Press, 1989).

Tanner, K., *God and Creation in Christian Theology: Tyranny or Empowerment* (Oxford: Blackwell, 1988).

Tate, A., 'An Ordinary Piece of Magic', in S. Groes and P. Childs (eds), *Julian Barnes* (New York: Continuum, 2011), pp. 51–68.

Taylor, C., *Sources of the Self* (Cambridge: Cambridge University Press, 1989).

Taylor, C., *A Secular Age* (Cambridge, MA: Harvard University Press, 2007).

Taylor, M., *Erring: a Postmodern Theology* (Chicago: University of Chicago Press, 1984).

Thomas, K., *Religion and the Decline of Magic* (London: Weidenfeld and Nicholson, 1971).

Tomalin, C., *Thomas Hardy: The Time-Torn Man* (London: Viking, 2006).

Tracey, T., *God, Action and Embodiment* (Grand Rapids: Eerdmans, 1984).

Tracey, T. (ed.), *The God Who Acts: Theological and Philosophical Explorations* (Grand Rapids: Eerdmans, 1994).

Vanhoozer, K., *Remythologizing Theology: Divine Action, Passion, and Authorship* (Cambridge: Cambridge University Press, 2010).

Ward, K., *Ethics and Christian Theology* (London: Allen & Unwin, 1970).

Webster, J., *Barth's Moral Theology: Human Action in Barth's Thought* (Edinburgh: T & T Clark, 1998).

Webster, J., 'The Grand Narrative of Jesus Christ: Barth's Christology', in G. Thompson and C. Moster (eds), *Karl Barth: A Future for Postmodern Theology?* (Hindmarsh: Australian Theological Forum, 2000), pp. 29–48.

Webster, J., 'On the Theology of Providence', in F. Murphy and P. Ziegler (eds), *The Providence of God* (Edinburgh: T & T Clark: 2009), pp. 158–78.

Wells, S., *Improvisation: The Drama of Theological Ethics* (London: SPCK, 2004).

White, V., *The Fall of a Sparrow: A Concept of Special Divine Action* (Exeter: Paternoster Press, 1985).

White, V., *Atonement and Incarnation* (Cambridge: Cambridge University Press, 1991).

White, V., *Paying Attention to People: An Essay on Individualism and Christian Belief* (London: SPCK, 1996).

White, V., *Life Beyond Death: Threads of Hope in Faith, Life and Theology* (London: Darton, Longman & Todd, 2006).

Wielenberg, E., *Value and Virtue in a Godless Universe* (Cambridge: Cambridge University Press, 2005).

Wilder, T., *The Bridge of San Luis Rey* (London: Penguin Classics, 2000).

Wiles, M., *Working Papers in Doctrine* (London: SCM Press, 1976).

Wiles, M., *God's Action in the World* (London: SCM Press, 1986).

Williams, R., 'Language, Reality and Desire in Augustine's De Doctrina', *Journal of Literature and Theology*, 3 (1989), pp. 138–50.

Williams, R., *On Christian Theology* (Oxford: Blackwell, 2000).

Williams, R., 'Redeeming Sorrows: Marilyn McCord Adams and the Defeat of Evil', in M. Higton (ed.), *Wrestling with Angels: Conversations in Modern Theology* (London: SCM Press, 2007), pp. 255–74.

Wright. N. T., *The Resurrection of the Son of God* (London: SPCK, 2004).

Yong, A., 'Divining "Divine Action" in Theology-Science', *Zygon*, 43 (2008), pp. 191–9.

Index

Lightning Source UK Ltd.
Milton Keynes UK
UKHW02f0516030718
325147UK00003B/114/P